ASEAN-U.S. Relations

The **Institute of Southeast Asian Studies (ISEAS)** was established as an autonomous organization in 1968. It is a regional centre dedicated to the study of socio-political, security and economic trends and developments in Southeast Asia and its wider geostrategic and economic environment. The Institute's research programmes are the Regional Economic Studies (RES, including ASEAN and APEC), Regional Strategic and Political Studies (RSPS), and Regional Social and Cultural Studies (RSCS).

ISEAS Publishing, an established academic press, has issued more than 2,000 books and journals. It is the largest scholarly publisher of research about Southeast Asia from within the region. ISEAS Publishing works with many other academic and trade publishers and distributors to disseminate important research and analyses from and about Southeast Asia to the rest of the world.

ASEAN-U.S. Relations
What Are the Talking Points?

Edited by
Pavin Chachavalpongpun

LSEAS

INSTITUTE OF SOUTHEAST ASIAN STUDIES
SINGAPORE

First published in Singapore in 2012 by
ISEAS Publishing
Institute of Southeast Asian Studies
30 Heng Mui Keng Terrace
Pasir Panjang
Singapore 119614
E-mail: publish@iseas.edu.sg
Website: http://bookshop.iseas.edu.sg

The responsibility for facts and opinions in this publication rests exclusively with the authors and their interpretations do not necessarily reflect the views or the policy of the Institute or its supporters.

ISEAS Library Cataloguing-in-Publication Data

ASEAN-U.S. relations : what are the talking points / edited by Pavin Chachavalpongpun.
   1.   Southeast Asia — Foreign relations — United States — Congresses.
   2.   United States — Foreign relations — Southeast Asia — Congresses.
   3.   ASEAN.
   4.   Regionalism — East Asia — Congresses.
   5.   Security, International — Southeast Asia — Congresses.
   6.   China — Foreign relations — United States — Congresses.
   7.   United States — Foreign relations — China — Congresses.
   8.   Burma — Foreign relations — United States — Congresses.
   9.   United States — Foreign relations — Burma — Congresses.
   I.   Pavin Chachavalpongpun.
   II. Institute of Southeast Asian Studies. ASEAN Studies Centre.
   III. Workshop on ASEAN-U.S. Relations : What are the Talking Points (2010 : Singapore)
DS525.9 A9A84   2012

ISBN 978-981-4311-55-7 (hard cover)
ISBN 978-981-4311-76-2 (e-book PDF)

Typeset by Superskill Graphics Pte Ltd
Printed in Singapore by Mainland Press Pte Ltd

CONTENTS

QUINTESSENTIAL ISSUES

TABLES AND FIGURES

PREFACE

This book is the result of a workshop of the ASEAN Studies Centre (ASC) held in July 2010. The primary objective is to raise important "talking points" in ASEAN-U.S. relations, in the hope that the workshop would produce a set of recommendations on how to improve their intricate ties. The ASC hopes that any findings as a result of this workshop would be considered by ASEAN in discussions at the subsequent ASEAN-U.S. Meeting and at other ASEAN-U.S. policy forums. We came up with three crucial themes: political cooperation, strategic issues, and economic and technical assistance between the United States and ASEAN. In each session, attention was paid to contemporary issues that have generated an impact on the ASEAN-U.S. relationship, such as maritime security, the U.S. military presence in this region, the inexorable relations between the United States and China and how both powers interact with ASEAN, the Myanmar issue, as well as the U.S. technical assistance, through the ASEAN Development Vision, to the Advance National Cooperation Programme, known as the ADVANCE project.

Ambassador K. Kesavapany, Director of the Institute of Southeast Asian Studies (ISEAS), earlier shared his thoughts on why the United States mattered to ASEAN and vice versa. His thoughts partly inspired the organization of this workshop. He encouraged the ASC to make this workshop a reality, stressing that it was time both ASEAN and the United States take their relationship more seriously than before, considering that the regional and international environment has greatly changed since the end of the Cold War. On behalf of Ambassador Rodolfo C. Severino, head of the ASC, we would like to sincerely thank Ambassador Kesavapany for his unfailing encouragement and support. We are grateful that Ambassador Kesavapany delivered the keynote speech at the workshop, highlighting the inseparable links between ASEAN and the United States.

This book is divided into two parts. The first part hosts a collection of essays which present an overview of ASEAN-U.S. relations. The second part contains papers which discuss specific issues presented by scholars and government officials during the workshop, plus a paper by Scot Marciel, Deputy Assistant Secretary of State of the United States, and U.S. Ambassador for ASEAN Affairs. This paper is based on his speech delivered at ISEAS on 9 December 2009 as part of the ASC's ASEAN Ambassadors Seminar Series.

The ASC would like to thank two other distinguished keynote speakers: Louis Mazel, Deputy Chief of Mission of the U.S. Embassy in Singapore, and Ambassador Minda Calaguian-Cruz of the Philippines Embassy in Singapore. Despite having just arrived in Singapore, Mazel agreed to give his keynote address on behalf of the U.S. Government. We are delighted to learn that his appearance at the workshop was his first official function on arriving in the city state. The ASC would like to thank Ambassador Cruz for representing the Philippines Government as the ASEAN country-coordinator for the United States. Appreciation also goes to all the paper presenters. I would particularly like to express my thanks to Michael Satin, Stephen C. Ma, Lam Peng Er, Neal Imperial, Jane Chan Git Yin, Michael Dembrosky, Yeong T. Pak, Patrick Kane, and Joshua Ho. I would also like to thank Ambassador Severino for contributing his short essay for inclusion in this volume and for spending his time to read the first draft of this manuscript, and Scot Marciel for allowing us to reproduce his speech in this publication. Last, but not least, I thank the East Asia Forum (EAF) for granting me permission to reproduce my article on ASEAN, the United States, and the East Asia Summit (EAS), in this book.

Pavin Chachavalpongpun
Editor

CONTRIBUTORS

Minda Calaguian-Cruz is Ambassador of the Philippines to Singapore.

Pavin Chachavalpongpun is Fellow and Lead Researcher for Political and Strategic Affairs, ASEAN Studies Centre, Institute of Southeast Asian Studies.

K. Kesavapany is Director of the Institute of Southeast Asian Studies.

Collin Koh Swee Lean is Associate Research Fellow at the Military Studies Program, Institute of Defence and Strategic Studies in the S. Rajaratnam School of International Studies (RSIS), Nanyang Technological University, Singapore.

Scot Marciel is U.S. Ambassador to Indonesia, former Deputy Assistant Secretary for Southeast Asia, and former U.S. Ambassador for ASEAN Affairs.

Louis Mazel is Deputy Chief of Mission, Embassy of the United States of America to Singapore.

Rodolfo C. Severino is Head of the ASEAN Studies Centre, Institute of Southeast Asian Studies.

U Myint Soe is a former Myanmar Diplomat. He was Visiting Senior Research Fellow, Institute of Southeast Asian Studies.

Ian Storey is Fellow and Editor of *Contemporary Southeast Asia*, Institute of Southeast Asian Studies.

Jennifer Collier Wilson is ASEAN Affairs Officer, USAID — Regional Development Mission for Asia.

Bo Zhiyue is Senior Research Fellow at the East Asian Institute of the National University of Singapore.

LIST OF ABBREVIATIONS

AADMER	ASEAN Agreement on Disaster Management and Emergency Response
ADM	ASEAN Data Model
ADMM	ASEAN Defence Ministers' Meeting
ADVANCE	ASEAN Development Vision to Advance National Cooperation and Economic Integration
AEP	ASEAN-U.S. Enhanced Partnership
AFTEX	ASEAN Federation of Textile Industries
AICHR	ASEAN Intergovernmental Commission on Human Rights
APC	Asia-Pacific Community
APSC	ASEAN Political-Security Community
APEC	Asia-Pacific Economic Cooperation
ARF	ASEAN Regional Forum
ASC	ASEAN Studies Centre
ASEAN	Association of Southeast Asian Nations
ASG	Abu Sayyaf Group
ASW	ASEAN Single Window
BBC	British Broadcasting Corporation
BTA	Bilateral Trade Agreement
CARAT	Cooperation Afloat Readiness and Training

COMLOGWESTPAC	Command Logistics Group Western Pacific
CSI	Container Security Initiative
DoC	ASEAN-China Declaration on the Conduct of Parties in the South China Sea
DoD	Department of Defense
DPRK	Democratic People's Republic of Korea
EAC	East Asia Community
EAF	East Asia Forum
EAS	East Asia Summit
EEZ	Exclusive Economic Zone
EPG	Eminent Persons Group
FTA	Free Trade Agreement
GWOT	Global War on Terror
G-20	Group of Twenty
HADR	Humanitarian and Disaster Relief
IAI	Initiative for ASEAN Integration
IPR	Intellectual Property Rights
ISEAS	Institute of Southeast Asian Studies
JI	Jemaah Islamiyah
MSP	Malacca Strait Patrols
NLD	National League for Democracy
NSWs	National Single Windows
NTS	Non-Traditional Security
PACOM	Pacific Command
PLAN	People's Liberation Army Navy
PMC	Post Ministerial Conference
PRC	People's Republic of China
PSI	Proliferation Security Initiative
QDR	Quadrennial Defense Review
RIMPAC	Rim of the Pacific
RMSI	Regional Maritime Security Initiative
SAFSA	Source ASEAN Full Service Alliance

SEACAT	Southeast Cooperation against Terrorism
SLD	Shangri-La Dialogue
SLOCs	Sea Lines of Communication
SME	Small and Medium Enterprises
SPDC	State Peace and Development Council
TAC	Treaty of Amity and Cooperation
TATF	Technical Assistance and Training Facility
TIFA	Trade and Investment Framework Arrangement
UNCTAD	United Nations Conference on Trade and Development
UNGA	United Nations General Assembly
UNSC	United Nations Security Council
UNSG	United Nations Secretary-General
UPOV	International Union for the Protection of New Varieties of Plants
USAID	U.S. Agency for International Development
USCG	United States Coast Guard
USN	The United States' Navy
WMD	Weapons of Mass Destruction
WTO	World Trade Organization

OVERVIEW

I

U.S. ENGAGEMENT WITH ASEAN[1]

K. Kesavapany

In November 2009 in Singapore, all the leaders of ASEAN met, for the first time in the organization's history, the President of the United States, Barack Obama. That historic meeting was another important milestone in the ASEAN-U.S. relationship.

The objective of this publication and of the workshop on which it is based is to illuminate the facts of those relations and the specific matter of the United States' engagement with ASEAN and East Asia, for possible use by ASEAN in discussions at the subsequent ASEAN-U.S. Summit Meeting and at other ASEAN-U.S. policy forums. The topics of discussion cover several elements of this relationship, ranging from the U.S. military presence in the ASEAN region, cooperation on maritime security, and recent U.S. policy towards Myanmar, to progress on economic and technical cooperation.

U.S. ENGAGEMENT WITH ASEAN

Since the ASEAN and American leaders met in 2009, many in Southeast Asia have believed that this was a new beginning in the United States' re-engagement with ASEAN. In recent years, although bilateral activities were carried out smoothly, some people in ASEAN faulted the United States for inattention to Southeast Asia at the highest leadership levels, noting that Secretary of State Condoleezza Rice's attendance at key meetings was very sporadic and that President George W. Bush was not a frequent visitor to the region. A "presidential presence" in the region was considered to be a necessary complement to diplomatic and trade initiatives.[2]

The United States' re-engagement with ASEAN would allow Washington to become directly involved in regional institutions. This would also enable the United States to become deeply involved in shaping the agendas of such groups. It would undoubtedly serve America's own interests far better in the longer term than its staying at the periphery. Economically, the United States continues to be a key export market for the ASEAN countries, but its importance has been falling just as China's has been increasing. The United States has also been the leading single-country investor in the region. ASEAN could do more to increase its attractiveness to American corporations by improving its trade and investment policies and practices. A cooperative ASEAN Economic Community (AEC) would create a strong incentive for American corporations to invest in ASEAN nations, which, in turn, would boost overall U.S.-ASEAN economic activity.[3]

On the security front, the United States has enjoyed very good relations with the governments of the region. This is partly because the United States has basically pursued a strategy of encouraging Southeast Asian nations to help themselves in combating domestic terrorist activities. Lately, the United States has paid greater attention to maritime security in the Malacca Strait, urging countries in the region to enhance their cooperative patrols. For Southeast Asia, the United States' military presence has been imperative in guaranteeing peace and security, especially when the regional environment has become somewhat unpredictable. The latest initiative of the ASEAN Defence Ministers' Meeting (ADMM) Plus Eight, which encompasses ASEAN's ten countries, plus China, Japan, South Korea, Australia,

New Zealand, India, Russia, and the United States, is another testament to how ASEAN values the indispensable security role of Washington in this region.

ASEAN AS THE REGION'S DRIVING FORCE

ASEAN's relations with the United States have evolved as the global system has changed. ASEAN is on its way to strengthening its political cohesion and economic integration by launching the ASEAN Charter and other measures, and assigning itself as an effective driving force for Asia-wide regional integration. Good and strong ties with the United States would permit ASEAN to maintain such a role. ASEAN's role as a hub for the many regional organizations in the Asia-Pacific is encouraged because ASEAN is considered a neutral player and an honest broker that brings together key regional powers, including the United States.

I do believe that this publication will bring to light new avenues of cooperation between ASEAN and the United States.

The Institute of Southeast Asian Studies (ISEAS) has cooperated with the East-West Centre (Washington Office) in a project aimed at highlighting the question of "why ASEAN matters to the United States and why the United States matters to ASEAN". A publication, *ASEAN Matters for America*, which is part of the project, gives a most detailed answer to this question. In addition to the printed copies, its text can be found at <http://www.eastwestcenter.org/> and <http://aseanmattersforamerica.org/>.

Notes

1. From the keynote address of K. Kesavapany, director of ISEAS, at the workshop on "ASEAN-U.S. Relations: What are the Talking Points?", organised by ISEAS on 16 July 2010.
2. At <http://www.eastwestcenter.org/news-center/east-west-wire/the-state-of-us-asean-relations/> (accessed 15 July 2010).
3. Ibid.

2

ASEAN-U.S. RELATIONS[1]

Louis Mazel

ASEAN has come a long way since its inception, and even since I was last working in Malaysia in the early 1990s. ASEAN has taken on an increasingly broad role in a wide array of regional and global issues, and the United States is determined to support ASEAN in its endeavours. We are committed to this area, and look forward to working with the organization even more closely in the coming years.

Back in 1967, when ASEAN was founded, there were only five members and the region was beset with serious differences and even conflict, but even then, the organization was key to bringing peace and stability to the region, offering a forum to discuss issues harmoniously. Today's ASEAN is ten members strong, at peace, and has formal relationships with many countries, and also with international organizations, including the United Nations and the G-20.[2] ASEAN has become the centrepiece of the construction of a regional architecture in the Asia-Pacific region, a central role that the United States supports.

The United States is fully committed to working with ASEAN. A prosperous and peaceful Southeast Asia has always been in our own interest, and ASEAN is and will continue to be the linchpin in bringing that vision to fruition. As ASEAN has changed over the years, so has our relationship. The United States has had a formal relationship with ASEAN since 1977, when the first ASEAN-U.S. Dialogue took place. Early discussions were focused primarily on economic issues, including trade and development. We have since added new areas for discussion, but the economic side remains a central part of our relationship, and I would like to highlight that.

Needless to say, trade holds a special place in the relationship. ASEAN members have pursued successful economic growth strategies centred on exports, many of which are destined for the 300-million-plus consumer market in the United States. The region's rapid economic development these past decades is a testament to the benefits of open trade. But the region is an important market for us as well, with over US$53 billion in our exports going to ASEAN countries last year. Taken together, the ASEAN countries are our fourth-largest export market. The Trade and Investment Framework Arrangement (TIFA) that we signed with ASEAN in 2006 has helped keep trade flowing. Trade took a beating last year as the economic downturn hit both sides, but I am happy to say that our exports to ASEAN are up 44 per cent so far this year (2010), and ASEAN's exports to us are up a still healthy 18 per cent. ASEAN is also a top destination for investment. American investment in ASEAN, at US$153 billion, is more than our commercial investments in China, Hong Kong, and Taiwan combined.

What we started here, we have now taken into new but equally important areas, working on transnational issues that are not just regional, but global in nature. At the inaugural U.S.-ASEAN leaders meeting in 2009, the leaders agreed to strengthen our cooperation to battle against terrorism and transnational crime. They also agreed to work on the impact of climate change, and we are aiding ASEAN's climate programme. In one major new area of cooperation, when he was in Singapore in June 2010, Defense Secretary Robert M.

Gates accepted Vietnam's invitation to attend the first ASEAN Defence Ministers Meeting Plus in October. We are also committed to improving food security by sharing best practices and building capacity. Our ASEAN office in Jakarta helped organize a conference on this topic in Singapore in June 2010. Cooperation in disaster management, the environment, and even human rights, is also in the offing.

So, we have a large number of issues to work on, but it's fair to ask, "Is the United States prepared to follow through on its commitments?" The answer is an emphatic "Yes". Never before have we had a president so personally committed to the region. Raised in Indonesia and Hawaii, President Barack Obama is often referred to as America's first Asia-Pacific president. President Obama travelled to Singapore in 2009 to attend the Asia-Pacific Economic Cooperation (APEC) meetings, and has committed not just once, but three times, to visit Indonesia.[3] Secretary of State Hillary Clinton has visited the region numerous times, including Hanoi in July 2010 for the ASEAN Regional Forum (ARF) meetings. Soon, we will have an ambassador to ASEAN posted in Jakarta, where the ASEAN Secretariat is headquartered.

The next question we have to ask is, "Can we do more?" As I mentioned earlier, ASEAN is ever increasing its capacity and, therefore, its role in global issues. As the ASEAN Community becomes a more respected voice in the world, its influence will grow. Our leaders have already discussed issues such as non-proliferation and disarmament, issues that transcend Southeast Asia. But challenges remain within ASEAN, particularly in encouraging the Myanmar leadership to pursue a more democratic path, a move that more than anything else would bring U.S.-ASEAN relations to a new level. On this and other challenges, the United States supports ASEAN's goals of contributing to solutions for the problems that still face the region and the world at large, and I wish to underscore my country's strong interest in partnering with ASEAN, not only in the traditional economic sphere, but on the full range of new transnational challenges we face in the twenty-first century.

Notes

1. Adapted from remarks by Louis Mazel, Deputy Chief of Mission, Embassy of the United States of America, Singapore.
2. The Group of Twenty (G-20) Finance Ministers and Central Bank Governors was established in 1999 to bring together systemically important industrialized and developing economies to discuss key issues in the global economy. Members include Argentina, Australia, Brazil, Canada, China, France, Germany, India, Indonesia, Italy, Japan, Mexico, Russia, Saudi Arabia, South Africa, the Republic of Korea, Turkey, the United Kingdom, the United States of America, and the European Union.
3. Finally, President Obama paid an official visit to Indonesia in November 2010.

3

DEVELOPMENTS IN ASEAN-U.S. RELATIONS[1]

Minda Calaguian-Cruz

At this stage in ASEAN–United States relations, we should thoroughly explore ways to expand those relations, which have been given a renewed impetus under the administration of President Barack Obama. We should also reflect on the current situations in global and regional affairs that impact on ASEAN-U.S. relations, and their implications for the future direction of this relationship. Among some of these concerns are the lingering impact of the recent global economic crisis and the threat of a possible double-dip recession emanating from the eurozone; the continuing, perhaps unending, war against terror; the fast pace of regional political as well as economic integration; and the increasing precariousness of the security situation in our region and among our neighbours.

OVERVIEW OF ASEAN-U.S. RELATIONS

Throughout the past three decades, ASEAN-U.S. relations have rapidly grown and expanded to cover a wide range of areas, including political security; economic, trade and investments; social and cultural; and development cooperation.

The principal focus of political-security cooperation has been the role of the United States in maintaining peace and stability in the region, including nuclear non-proliferation, counterterrorism, combating transnational crime, and the situation in Northeast Asia, including the Korean Peninsula. Recently, ASEAN leaders have talked about the evolving regional architecture and the United States' possible future participation in such a regional arrangement. There are indications that the United States is interested in following the discussions on the evolving regional architecture and recognizes ASEAN's central role as a driving force in any form of regional architecture that is being discussed. The United States, nonetheless, actively participates in existing regional cooperation frameworks, such as the ASEAN Regional Forum (ARF). ASEAN welcomed the United States' accession to the Treaty of Amity and Cooperation (TAC) in Southeast Asia during the Post Ministerial Conference (PMC) in July 2009. This is another signal of the United States' renewed vigour in its engagement with ASEAN, particularly in the security field.

ASEAN-U.S. economic cooperation is based on the ASEAN-U.S. Trade and Investment Framework Arrangement, which is a non-binding set of parameters and activities jointly implemented by ASEAN and the United States to promote better trade and investment flows. It may be noted that the United States is among the last of ASEAN's ten dialogue partners that still do not have a legally binding free trade agreement (FTA) with ASEAN, perhaps owing to differing economic policies and priorities between the two.

On sociocultural and development cooperation, the focus by the United States is on educational exchanges, the environment, science and technology, and disaster risk reduction and response.

THE PHILIPPINES AS COUNTRY COORDINATOR: ACHIEVEMENTS TO DATE

The Philippines is honoured to serve as country coordinator for ASEAN-U.S. Dialogue Relations from 2009 to 2012. The Philippines has historically been at the crossroads of Asia and America, and we shall continue our role as a bridge across the Pacific for a strengthened ASEAN-U.S. relationship. In our role as country coordinator for ASEAN-U.S. relations, we shall serve as an effective conduit through which positive and meaningful exchanges shall occur between all ASEAN member states and the United States.

We were certainly off to a good start as country coordinator, firing off with the first historic ASEAN-U.S. Leaders' Meeting that finally took place in Singapore in November 2009, after more than thirty years of partnership. We thank our friends from Singapore for generously hosting that meeting, and Thailand as ASEAN Chair that year, as well as all our ASEAN and American partners in making that historic event a great success.

We have subsequently endeavoured to push our partnership forward through the various activities undertaken in the year since we took over from Singapore the tasks of country coordinator in July 2009, guided by the directions given to us by our leaders at their first meeting, and inspired by President Obama's policy pronouncement of a reinvigorated United States' engagement with ASEAN under his administration. In the first year of our term as country coordinator, we undertook the following significant steps to push forward the momentum of a reinvigorated ASEAN-U.S. partnership.

First, we convened the Special ASEAN-U.S. Senior Officials' Meeting in November 2009, just three weeks prior to the first ASEAN-U.S. Leaders Meeting, specifically to draft the joint statement that was to become the main outcome document of that first leaders' meeting.

Second, we led the crafting of the new "Plan of Action to Implement the Joint Vision on Enhanced Partnership" to cover the years 2011 to 2016. The current plan of action is set to expire in July 2011, and the ASEAN-U.S. leaders tasked the Philippines to lead in crafting the new plan.

Third, the Philippines, through the ASEAN Committee on Science and Technology, is pushing forward the negotiations for the ASEAN-U.S. Agreement on Science and Technology Cooperation, from where Singapore left off at the end of its term as country coordinator.

Fourth, we shepherded the negotiation for the terms of reference of the ASEAN-U.S. Eminent Persons Group (EPG). The creation of the EPG was proposed by President Obama during the first leaders' meeting to provide guidance on the future long-term directions of the partnership.

Fifth, at the technical level, the Philippine Permanent Representative in Jakarta convened the ASEAN-U.S. Working Group and the ASEAN-U.S. Joint Cooperation Committee to review the progress of cooperation between the two sides and to continue drafting the new plan of action. Also, the Philippines permanent representative in Jakarta led ASEAN in discussing the new programmes of U.S. assistance to ASEAN under the ASEAN-U.S. Technical Assistance and Training Facility (TATF) and the ASEAN Development Vision to Advance National Cooperation and Economic Integration (ADVANCE).

Sixth, in April 2010, an ASEAN Economic Ministers' Trade and Investment Roadshow was undertaken in the United States. In May 2010, we successfully convened the 23rd ASEAN-U.S. Dialogue in Manila, where our senior officials agreed on important steps to push forward the implementation of our leaders' directives in the joint statement of their first meeting in November.

Last, but not least, a draft programme for consultations and meetings in the United States of the ASEAN Intergovernmental Commission on Human Rights (AICHR) was prepared by the United States for consideration by AICHR representatives.

FUTURE DIRECTIONS: ASEAN-U.S. PRIORITIES
FOR COOPERATION

At the 42nd ASEAN-U.S. Senior Officials' Dialogue in Washington DC in 2009, both sides agreed to adopt a number of priorities for cooperation.

In the political security arena, the priorities include transnational crime, the threat of terrorism, capacity building for good governance, enhancement of rule of law and judiciary systems, and human rights promotion. In the economic domain, the focus is on initiatives to promote intellectual property rights protection, the use of internationally adopted standards, the increased transparency and simplification of rules and procedures, collaboration to support ASEAN small and medium enterprises (SMEs), information and communications technology, and finance cooperation. As for sociocultural cooperation, the leaders agreed to promote the development of science and technology; disaster management, including capacity-building programmes to improve ASEAN's capability to prevent, respond to, and recover from the impact of, natural disasters; health cooperation, including the threat of emerging infectious diseases; climate change; food and energy security; education, and the setting up of scholarship funds and training programmes.

The 1st ASEAN-U.S. Leaders' Meeting in November 2009 also set the following as immediate priorities for cooperation:

- Consultations between the U.S. Energy Department and its ASEAN counterparts on energy cooperation, particularly in clean and renewable energy;
- Consultations between the U.S. Defense Minister and his ASEAN counterparts to discuss security cooperation. In line with this, the United States would be invited by the ASEAN defence ministers to participate in the first session of the ASEAN Defence Ministers Meeting Plus Eight (ADMM+8), in which the ASEAN ministers would meet with their counterparts from

eight dialogue partners, including the United States, for the very first time in a formal setting;

- The creation of the ASEAN-U.S. Eminent Persons Group, as mentioned earlier. It is expected that this group will be formally launched at the 2nd ASEAN-U.S. Leaders' Meeting later in 2010;[2]
- The establishment of the U.S. Mission to ASEAN in Jakarta;
- The drafting of the programme of activities for the visit of the AICHR to the United States in November 2010; and
- Cooperation to promote educational exchanges, science and technology, trade and investments liberalization, combating terrorism and transnational crime, health, people/labour mobility, environment and climate change, clean energy, food security, nuclear non-proliferation, and support towards the attainment of the Millennium Development Goals.

The recent signing and implementation of the ASEAN Charter, as well as the adoption by the ASEAN leaders of the three ASEAN blueprints — Political Security, Economic, and Socio-Cultural — and the 2nd Workplan of the Initiative for ASEAN Integration (IAI), are ASEAN's main road maps towards the attainment of the envisioned ASEAN Community by 2015. It is, therefore, imperative that the plans, programmes, and projects set out in the new plan of action are in consonance with the action lines of the three blueprints and the IAI Workplan II. This will ensure that future ASEAN-U.S. cooperation is directed at supporting the attainment of the envisioned ASEAN Community 2015.

At the moment, the permanent representatives in Jakarta, together with the U.S. Mission there, are drafting the new plan of action for the period 2011 to 2016. The above mentioned priorities for cooperation are the focus of the new plan. As it is still very much a work in progress, we could not as yet provide full details of the new plan. We shall wait until the permanent representatives are finished with this task by the end of 2010. The new plan of action is to be approved by the ministers at the 44th ASEAN Ministerial Meeting and Post Ministerial Conferences in July 2011.

Finally, the structure and substance of future ASEAN-U.S. cooperation will continue to be guided by the 2005 Joint Vision Statement on ASEAN-U.S. Enhanced Partnership, but moulded by new and future challenges in the regional and global arena that may affect the course of our partnership over the next decades. Serious new challenges, such as the fragile recovery from the 2008 global economic crisis; the threat of double-dip recession triggered by heavily indebted developed economies; the impact of climate change on the environment and natural disasters; emerging health pandemics; terrorism, particularly nuclear terrorism; transnational crime, including maritime piracy, among others, will certainly drive specific modes of cooperation and should be taken into consideration in charting the future course of the ASEAN-U.S. partnership.

Note

1. Remarks by Ambassador Minda Calaguian-Cruz of the Philippines to Singapore. Ambassador Cruz was invited to deliver her remarks as a representative of her government since the Philippines is currently country coordinator for the ASEAN-U.S. Dialogue.
2. The ASEAN-U.S. Eminent Persons Group was created on 24 September 2010.

4

THE UNITED STATES, RUSSIA TO BE PART OF EAST ASIA SUMMIT

Rodolfo C. Severino

Towards the end of October 2010, the heads of government of the Association of Southeast Asian Nations (ASEAN) gathered in Hanoi for the second time that year, as called for in the new ASEAN Charter. Afterwards, they met with their counterparts, collectively and individually, from China, Japan and South Korea in the context of ASEAN Plus Three, and then with the Prime Minister of India. They then sat down with the leaders of Australia, China, India, Japan, Korea, and New Zealand in the annual East Asia Summit (EAS). What was different from previous EAS was that the Russian Foreign Minister, Sergei Lavrov, and the U.S. Secretary of State, Hillary Rodham Clinton, were in attendance, representing their respective leaders "as special guests of the Chair".

One of the most momentous decisions that the EAS leaders made was to "invite the Russian Federation and the United States of America, given their expressed interest in and commitment to the EAS process, to join the EAS in 2011", having before them the recommendation of their foreign ministers.

In July 2009, the ASEAN foreign ministers had their annual meeting in Hanoi, Vietnam's capital. They then convened with ministers of the major powers and others from the Asia-Pacific in the ASEAN Regional Forum (ARF), the only region-wide ministerial-level forum for the discussion of political and security issues. The ASEAN ministers also met with their counterparts in an ASEAN Plus Three setting and had informal consultations with those of the other members of the EAS.

Easily one of the most noteworthy subjects of these gatherings was the prospect of Russia's and the United States' future participation in the region's rapidly evolving and increasingly complex political configuration, economic relationships, and transnational cooperation through their membership in the EAS. According to their chairman's statement, the EAS ministers' "informal consultations ... welcomed the expressed interest of the Russian Federation and the United States to join the East Asia Summit (EAS) and supported ASEAN's decision on the matter". The ministers are said to have "noted" that the ASEAN ministers would recommend to the ASEAN leaders at their Hanoi summit in October that they "formally" invite Russia and the United States to join the EAS. For their part, the ARF ministers "noted" the ASEAN ministers' welcome to "the expressed interest" of Russia and the United States to join the EAS and their stated recommendation that the October ASEAN summit formally invite them to do so. Both statements stressed that the invitation should be issued "with appropriate arrangements and timing".

In an encounter with the media after the ASEAN Ministerial Meeting on 20 July 2010, George Yeo, then Singapore's Foreign Minister, explained that the ASEAN ministers had asked their senior officials to work out the "modalities" of Russian and American participation in the EAS. It would clearly not be so simple. Minister Yeo emphasized that the officials would have to "safeguard" the EAS' current agenda and priorities, including a free trade area and regional connectivity, both of which were under study and discussion by the group. He stressed the importance of ASEAN's centrality in the EAS process, that the process should continue to be ASEAN-led, and that the EAS would continue to take place every year in the ASEAN region. The five "priority areas" of EAS cooperation are finance, energy, education, the prevention of avian influenza, and disaster management.

A number of issues surrounding the envisioned American and Russian membership in the EAS remain to be worked out. What would happen to the EAS, for example, if the American or Russian leader found himself unable to travel to Southeast Asia for an EAS meeting? Could the EAS' character as a leaders-led forum and its strategic agenda be maintained if Washington or Moscow, both global powers, found it necessary, for domestic political or foreign-policy considerations, to inject its own national or global interests into the EAS process? Would U.S. participation in the EAS not further complicate attempts to conclude an EAS-wide free trade agreement in the form of the proposed Comprehensive Economic Partnership for East Asia (CEPEA) in the light of the U.S. difficulty in getting the free trade deal with South Korea ratified? Or would it hasten negotiations on the Trans-Pacific Partnership initiated by Singapore, Brunei Darussalam, New Zealand, and Chile, which the United States has evinced interest in pushing and joining?

In an attempt to address these questions, proposals for an ASEAN Plus Eight summit — the eight being the six current EAS participants, Russia, and the United States — have been floated. This arrangement would be in place of the more formal and stringent American and Russian membership in the annual EAS. In any case, the "expressed interest" of both Washington and Moscow in EAS membership indicates their determination to deepen their engagement in a region of the world that is rapidly growing in political and economic importance and is fast developing as a shaper of world affairs. It also manifests their desire to continue benefiting from that growth and to ensure that they take part in the process of forming the region's political and economic configuration.

At the same time, the positive Asia-Pacific reception of that interest has expressed Asia's recognition of the United States' and Russia's importance to ASEAN, East Asia, and the Asia-Pacific as a whole. Most East Asian capitals consider the United States' strategic military presence in the area as a critical factor in regional security and stability.

Despite its current economic difficulties, the United States remains a leading market and source of investments for East Asia. It is at the cutting edge of industrial and military technology. It continues to exert considerable economic and political heft, regionally as well as globally. Its mass media continue to shape public perceptions of Asia-Pacific affairs.

Russia, on the other hand, has the second-largest nuclear arsenal in the world, after the United States. Like the United States, it is a permanent member of the United Nations Security Council, with the power of veto. Much of its vast land area is located in Asia. It has enormous energy and other resources for exploitation or importation by Asia that is hungry for them. Moscow has been knocking on the EAS door since its inception in 2005.

There is thus a common desire all round for Russia and the United States to be part of the process of regionalization in this part of the world. In this light, it seems certain that the American and Russian leaders will be present at the next EAS, to be held in conjunction with the ASEAN Summit later in the year, in Bali in November 2011. The ASEAN and EAS decision on this indicates that the Americans' — and Russians' — interest in and right of participation in Asia-Pacific affairs have been recognized and accepted by the other major actors of the region.

5

HOW DOES THE UNITED STATES PLAY INTO THE EAST ASIA SUMMIT FOR ASEAN?[1]

Pavin Chachavalpongpun

Members of the Association of Southeast Asian Nations (ASEAN) have agreed to invite the United States and Russia to participate in the region-wide forum, the East Asia Summit (EAS), which encompasses ASEAN Plus Six: Japan, China, South Korea, Australia, New Zealand, and India. The invitation immediately met with a favourable response from Kurt Campbell, U.S. Assistant Secretary of State for East Asia and the Pacific, emphasizing the United States' renewed interest in its relations with Southeast Asia.

It is generally believed that United States' participation will minimize China's increasing domination of the EAS. Long years of U.S. disengagement with ASEAN, particularly during the Bush administration, allowed China to take a leading role in ASEAN-led regional platforms. This situation coincided with the rise of China, both economically and militarily.

Over the years, China worked to erase its image as a threat. The popular catchphrase "China's peaceful rise" is frequently heard as

Beijing does business with its Southeast Asian neighbours. But the territorial disputes in the South China Sea have effectively damaged this peace-loving image. The United States' re-engagement with the region, through EAS, could be employed to counterbalance China's military might. In other words, the United States is needed and is urged to resume its Cold War role as a security guarantor for countries in Southeast Asia.

And what does China really think about the United States' admission into the EAS? Madam Xue Hanqin, China's Ambassador to ASEAN, once provocatively asked, "Why do many Southeast Asians talk about the United States' re-engagement with ASEAN when in fact the United States has never actually left the region?" Despite her sarcasm, China has at times signalled that it also wanted the United States "to be around" in the region, particularly to ensure that Japan remains "demilitarized". Bitter history and mutual distrust remain forceful elements in Northeast Asian international politics.

ASEAN has been aware of emerging concepts of regional architectures and feared its relevance could be diminished. Japan's idea of an East Asia Community (EAC) and Australia's Asia-Pacific Community (APC) posed serious threats to the very existence of ASEAN. Would ASEAN lose its competitiveness in a world replete with new regional organizations? Former Australian Prime Minister Kevin Rudd's initiative of the APC threatened to lessen ASEAN influence. In defending itself, the group was willing to take great pains to question the APC concept, including employing regional media to rebuke Rudd's idea of disintegrating the region, rather than integrating it.

Hence, the invitation extended to the United States to attend the EAS can be perceived as a part of ASEAN's plot to retain its centric role in Southeast Asia and beyond. ASEAN recognizes that the Obama administration has shifted its policy towards Southeast Asia. "ASEAN is the most successful regional forum in Southeast Asia and it provides a legitimate channel for the United States to play its role", said one ASEAN diplomat.

Not all members of the EAS are ecstatic about the admission of the United States. Myanmar, for one, is not too keen about having the United States around in the region. True, Washington has remodified its position vis-à-vis Naypyidaw. But U.S. sanctions have not been dismantled. The U.S. Government has been critical of the election in Myanmar held in November 2010, which it considered a charade. Some ASEAN members are trying to downplay Myanmar's discontentment with the United States' involvement in EAS, offering a more upbeat outlook and claiming the EAS could be used as an extra avenue for Washington and Naypyidaw to "get to know" each other better.

Overall, the U.S. membership of the EAS serves to fulfil ASEAN's fundamental objectives, both to engage with outside powers, and to strengthen its position as the core organization in Southeast Asia. For Washington, its involvement in the EAS will not be merely symbolic, but may assist in transforming ASEAN from a known talk shop, as often described by its critics, to a substance-based forum.

Note

1. This article first appeared in the East Asia Forum website on 17 August 2010 <http://www.eastasiaforum.org/2010/08/17/how-the-us-plays-into-the-east-asia-summit-for-asean/>. The author would like to thank the East Asia Forum for granting the permission to reproduce this article.

QUINTESSENTIAL ISSUES

6

A NEW ERA IN THE LONG-STANDING U.S.-ASEAN RELATIONSHIP[1]

Scot Marciel

The United States and the Association of Southeast Asian Nations (ASEAN) have entered a new era in our relations. I would like to discuss the current relationship and what we hope that relationship will look like in the coming years. I do not want to emphasize too much our past relations with ASEAN, but it is important to devote some lines to recounting how long-standing our commitment to ASEAN has been.

I want to emphasize three points that came out of what President Obama said to the ASEAN leaders when he met with them in Singapore in November 2009. First, the President reminded people both in his speech in Tokyo and in his Singapore meeting that the United States is a Pacific power, and we have been committed to and engaged with Southeast Asia in a serious way for decades. In recent years, there has been a little buzz that even those of us in Washington could hear from ten thousand miles away, expressing some concerns that the United States was distracted or perhaps not fully committed to ASEAN and to Southeast Asia. And it was a source of some frustration for all of us working in ASEAN, because we felt we have actually been quite active. We can debate on that point, but the important thing is that the perception did exist that the United States was not as engaged as it should be.

The ASEAN–United States Dialogue relationship began thirty-two years ago, in 1977, during a very different time globally. Our early relations with ASEAN were focused on economics, trade, and development. It was not until the 11th ASEAN–U.S. Dialogue meeting in Brunei in 1993 that we even had any political issues for discussion on our formal dialogue agenda. Then, in 2002, we established the ASEAN Cooperation Plan, and Secretary of State Colin Powell signed the ASEAN–United States of America Joint Declaration for Cooperation to Combat International Terrorism. By then, the world had changed, and ASEAN–U.S. relations were changing in response. Our relations have grown dramatically since then. ASEAN leaders and President Bush issued the Joint Vision Statement in 2005, creating the Enhanced Partnership, and ASEAN foreign ministers and Secretary of State Condoleezza Rice signed the plan of action to implement that statement in 2006. We also signed the Trade and Investment Framework Arrangement that year. As we implemented those agreements, our work with the ASEAN Secretariat and with member-government officials increased greatly.

My own position reflects this broader engagement. In May of 2008, I became the first United States Ambassador for ASEAN Affairs. The establishment of this position demonstrated the broad recognition in the U.S. Congress as well as the administration of the importance of ASEAN–U.S. ties. Through the end of 2008, we worked closely and effectively with the ASEAN Secretariat and all of the ASEAN nations to support ASEAN's goals and to strengthen our ties. But I think it is fair to say that this year has seen a major boost in our relations.

First, on the ASEAN side, a new charter was put in place. It entered into force on 15 December 2008. Since then, the building of numerous regional institutions to manage security, economic, human rights, and many other issues where we have common interests is well under way. On the U.S. side, Secretary of State Hillary Clinton made several trips to the region since taking office in January 2009, a remarkable level of engagement. In February 2009, she was the first secretary of state and the first U.S. government cabinet member to visit the ASEAN Secretariat. In July, Secretary Clinton signed the Treaty of Amity and Cooperation (TAC). She also announced that the United States would establish a mission to the ASEAN Secretariat in Jakarta.

As we all know, President Obama finally met with ASEAN leaders in Singapore in November 2009, the first time that has happened. I wish it had happened sooner, but I am glad that it happened now. This first meeting of a U.S. president with all ten ASEAN leaders is a clear indication of a new era in our political engagement. The President also said that the United States is committed to engaging ASEAN at the highest levels and proposed that he meet with ASEAN leaders again in 2010. Thus, in the first year of the Obama administration, we saw, not only in words but in practice, a very strong reaffirmation of the U.S. commitment to ASEAN and to Southeast Asia.

The second point, and this is a long-standing one but one that has been reinforced by the current administration, is about U.S. support for ASEAN's success. What has driven this long-standing engagement and recent efforts to boost relations to an even higher level? First and foremost, the United States has long recognized that a strong, prosperous, and peaceful Southeast Asia was in its national interest, and that a successful ASEAN could and would contribute to that goal. If Southeast Asia is successful, meaning prosperous, and its people enjoy peace, stability, and increased opportunity, that's good for the United States, it is good for the region, it is good for us. Therefore, we have always supported ASEAN's goals, and we clearly support ASEAN's very ambitious agenda of building a community by 2015, including economic integration and a single market. The President stressed in all his conversations in Singapore that we support that both rhetorically and in practice. We have a number of assistance programmes with the ASEAN Secretariat and ASEAN as a whole to try to help ASEAN achieve these goals; things such as capacity building for the secretariat, workshops, and seminars to identify some barriers to the integration of ASEAN. Thus, in this sense, the U.S. agenda for ASEAN is, in fact, the ASEAN agenda. We do not have an agenda other than to support ASEAN's ambitious goals. That is why we have been working with ASEAN — as well as bilaterally with ASEAN members — for decades.

The third point is a little bit new. For a long time when we worked with ASEAN we talked about strengthening ASEAN's important role and tried to work together more. We continue to do that, of course, but the important third point is that we see what ASEAN has done in recent years. We see the work of the Eminent Persons Group. We see the work to build and ratify the Charter, to create a legal status for ASEAN, to create the blueprints for integration, and to build communities in the three pillars of ASEAN. We see ASEAN playing an important role in the region and in the world, and we agree. Therefore, let us be partners. We look at ASEAN not only as an institution that is doing work in Southeast Asia, but as a regional and global partner. Some might think that this is a little bit ambitious, but I think it is essential.

We recognize and appreciate ASEAN's significant development and progress in recent years and have worked to respond positively to it. ASEAN's Charter, its Intergovernmental Commission on Human Rights, the development of a community with its three pillars — all are of interest to the United States and to ASEAN's other dialogue partners. These political developments alone would keep us interested in and supportive of the community-building process. We see ASEAN becoming a more regional and global player. The President said, "Let us work together, let us work together for climate change, let us work together in supporting the G20 and promoting global recovery and long-term development, let us work together on trade, let us work together on non-proliferation, whether it is North Korea, Iran or broader non-proliferation issues." I think this is going to be a work in progress for a while. We and ASEAN are trying to figure out how we can work together as diplomatic partners. It goes without saying that, while ASEAN has made a lot of progress, it does not yet always speak with one voice or has one person who can speak as a spokesperson for ASEAN for all its foreign policy issues, but I think it is moving in that direction, and we are very interested in being a partner.

That partnership is going to work on issues that are of concern to both the United States and ASEAN — climate change, economic growth, economic development and trade — and not just the issues that the United States cares about, not just the issues that ASEAN cares about. This is the area where we have a lot of work to do. We also have work to do dealing with each other as partners on issues that affect individual ASEAN countries, issues such as Myanmar, internal ASEAN issues. It is a problem for the people of the country, it is a problem for ASEAN, it is a problem for the United States, and we need to find ways we can work together as diplomatic partners. It is not going to be easy, but I think it is very important. Again, ASEAN sets the agenda; it is a very impressive agenda and we very much welcome it. I meet regularly with my ASEAN counterparts and we meet at different levels to talk about how the United States can be helpful.

ASEAN is also an important economic partner for the United States, and vice versa. We have known this since the beginning of our dialogue relationship. Commercial interests on both sides would be sufficient to drive our cooperation. ASEAN-U.S. trade totalled US$180 billion in 2008, growing in a difficult year. What may be less well known is the story on investment. The American private sector has accumulated US$153 billion in foreign direct investment in ASEAN, on what is called a historical-cost basis. For the last two years, the cumulative American investment in ASEAN has been greater than our combined total investment in China, Japan, and Korea (which was US$152 billion in 2008). ASEAN is now the destination for the fifth largest share of U.S. foreign investment in the world. Very few people know that; very few people in the United States know it.

There may be a temptation to call this extraordinary level of economic engagement between the United States and ASEAN a success and to put some of the problems raised by the private sector, which are limiting an even greater investment relationship, on the back burner. But just the opposite tack is called for. Doesn't it make sense for us to do all we can to maximize one of the strongest features of our relationship? When we consider that this investment is not just dollar signs, but that it is actually the conveyor belt for trade growth, foreign exchange earnings, technology transfer, and broad economic development, we have a common interest in making sure that these benefits are all they can be, especially as ASEAN implements its plans to become a single market and production base.

President Obama cited our economic relations and more when he met with ASEAN leaders in November 2009. He described his own experience in Southeast Asia as proof that the ASEAN countries and their 560 million people have very close and personal links with communities and families in the United States. Building on those many individual relationships, the President described the United States not simply as a partner for ASEAN, but as a member of the ASEAN family. We have a relationship that will support ASEAN's development, advance the ambitious goals for the region that we share, and result in great benefits for Southeast Asia and beyond.

The President and ASEAN leaders issued a Joint Declaration when they met in November 2009 that describes a number of actions we will take in the coming months. I think it will be useful to review the main points of the Joint Declaration:

- One action will be the establishment of an Eminent Persons Group to help define the road ahead and to generate ideas for enhanced ASEAN–U.S. cooperation in addressing regional and global issues. The Eminent Persons Group was established in September 2010.

• The Joint Declaration recognizes the importance of educational and professional exchanges, especially in science and technology and people-to-people interactions. We plan to pursue the conclusion of a science and technology agreement with ASEAN. We will increase opportunities for English language training in response to the many requests we have received from ASEAN officials. We will also be discussing people/labour mobility, interfaith dialogue, and development cooperation.

• The leaders agreed on a vision for building a regional architecture that is inclusive, promotes shared values and norms, and respects diversity in the region, with ASEAN as central in the process. The United States will be looking closely at existing institutions and all the ideas for regional architecture that have been proposed. We will consult with our ASEAN colleagues as this process moves forward.

• Human rights were discussed by the leaders. The President invited members of the ASEAN Intergovernmental Commission on Human Rights to the United States to consult with international experts in this field. In addition, we are supporting a human rights resource centre for ASEAN, a Track II initiative with the University of Indonesia as its host institution, and including a network of universities throughout ASEAN.

• We welcomed the ASEAN leaders' statement on connectivity, which they adopted at their October 2009 summit meeting. We will be consulting with ASEAN's other partners and our private sector, who are active in this area.

• ASEAN welcomed continued U.S. participation in regional institutions that deal with security such as the ASEAN Regional Forum, and also welcomed the plans of our Secretary of Defense to consult with his ASEAN counterparts on the proposed ASEAN Defense Ministers' Meeting Plus mechanism.

- The ASEAN and U.S. leaders noted the vibrant economic relations that ASEAN and the United States currently enjoy and called for additional cooperation, including under the TIFA (Trade and Investment Framework Arrangement). The U.S. Government is discussing an idea with the U.S–ASEAN Business Council to invite the ten ASEAN Trade Ministers to a roadshow in the United States in 2011. This would be an opportunity for a policy dialogue between ASEAN and U.S. officials and the business community. Most important, it will be an opportunity to showcase the opportunities presented by ASEAN economic integration and the large and prosperous market it will create. The ASEAN Economic Community has tremendous potential to be a game changer: it will transform the way the world perceives ASEAN. I was pleased to be able to participate in the launching of the book, *Realizing the ASEAN Economic Community*, while I was in Singapore attending the Leaders Meeting. The goal of the ASEAN Economic Community is to create a free flow of goods, services, foreign direct investment, and skilled labour, as well as a freer flow of capital in the region. This will be technically and politically difficult. But the book, which was produced by ASEAN and the United States, and published by the Institute of Southeast Asian Studies (ISEAS), quantifies the likely benefits of the Economic Community. It convincingly estimates that the effects will be very large, even greater than the effects of the single market in Europe. Trade in goods, foreign investment, per capita income, progress in narrowing the development gap and in consumer markets, will all see improvements.
- Our leaders agreed to strengthen efforts to combat international crime and terrorism. Our technical officials will be discussing with ASEAN officials a number of areas of possible cooperation beginning right away.
- The leaders agreed to work closely together on climate change. As a result, we are assigning a climate advisor to the ASEAN

Secretariat to aid in the advancement of ASEAN's climate programme. The President also offered to have Secretary of Energy Steven Chu meet with ASEAN Energy Ministers to discuss energy security and clean energy initiatives.

- The leaders agreed to strengthen cooperation on food security, particularly to promote investment, capacity building, and best practices. We will be consulting with ASEAN and the private sector on implementing this initiative.

- While the United States and ASEAN have an active programme of disaster management activities, the leaders emphasized the importance of further strengthening cooperation in this area. The United States will continue to support ASEAN capacity building to deal more effectively with disasters. We will provide additional support for the recently ratified ASEAN Agreement on Disaster Management and Emergency Response (AADMER) and will cooperate with ASEAN in the development of a multi-hazard early warning system.

ASEAN has twin challenges on the economic integration front. One is carrying out the economic integration work, which is a huge challenge. Imagine an ASEAN in 2015 that is a single market; imagine what that is going to do to the region. I think it is huge, and I am surprised that people are not talking even more about it; but it is not going to be easy. We all know it is easy to talk about political things, about diplomatic things. It is easy to talk about economic integration, but much harder to do. It is a huge challenge that requires an extraordinary political leadership from within ASEAN. The United States and others will be supportive, but it is going to require very strong leadership from all of ASEAN.

The other part of the challenge is the marketing challenge. People in the United States and businesses in the United States for the most part do not know what ASEAN is trying to do. You will be surprised how little people know about ASEAN, not just in the United States, but also in Europe and other parts of the world. There has not been much marketing about ASEAN, especially the economic integration. I think it is a challenge and also an opportunity, because there is a great story to tell out there. The opportunity to attract significant interest and significant investments, create jobs, reduce poverty, increase wealth in this region, is dramatic. One of the things we have to do is to help ASEAN do a better job of marketing itself, while it does the harder job of achieving economic integration. I have gone on at length about the economic pillar, but I think it is really important, and ASEAN only has until 2015 to achieve the goal. I think a lot of things have been done, but this has to be a top priority and the one we need to continue to focus on.

There is another paragraph in the Joint Declaration that may not stand out at first glance and has no action items to be checked off in its language. However, its implications are large and, in a nutshell, it describes the new level of ASEAN-U.S. relations we are working to build. This is the discussion of ASEAN's growing capacity and role in global issues. It will not always be easy to step up to the plate, as they say in the United States. But, as ASEAN implements its own community, its voice will be increasingly sought out and listened to in the world community. Already, ASEAN is an official observer at the United Nations, is developing formal relations with other regional organizations, and has participated in meetings of the G-20. The President and ASEAN leaders discussed non-proliferation and disarmament, North Korea, and other global issues that extend beyond Southeast Asia. The United States will support ASEAN's continuing role in addressing multilateral issues consistent with its growing capacity to make a contribution to the problems facing the international community. I would add that, as the United States increases its engagement with ASEAN, we hope that the ASEAN countries will increase their support of the institution as well. The ASEAN Secretariat is too under-resourced and staffed to manage the global role that the organization must assume. I would encourage ASEAN countries and other partner-nations to dedicate the much needed personnel and resources to create the capacity for ASEAN to fulfil its important mandate.

I mentioned other issues. I mentioned the Charter. I should mention the new human rights body. I think it is a positive step. I know there has been a lot of criticism that it does not go far enough. It is almost impossible to go far enough when it comes to human rights. You always need to do more, so I would say this is not a satisfactory step, but it is a positive step, it is a first step. Five years ago human rights was not on the agenda at all in ASEAN. It is on the agenda now with a new commission. I think it is a good step, and we will be supportive. The President has invited all human rights commissioners to come to the United States. It is like so many other things in developing regional organizations. We start with one step and then we build from there. Without saying that it meets all of our ambitious goals, I would say it is important and a positive step.

Now, a word or two about Myanmar. Many of you know that Secretary Clinton announced early this year that we would do a review of our policy towards Myanmar, because the policy we had been following had not worked. The second part of what she said does not get as much echo as it should. She said that the ASEAN policy of engagement also has not worked. So we have to try something new, a different approach. We did an extensive review and came up with an approach. It is not a revolutionary shift, but rather, adds some tools to our diplomatic arsenal, including an effort at direct dialogue between the United States and Myanmar officials. We did the first round in New York and then Kurt Campbell (Assistant Secretary of State for East Asian and Pacific Affairs), my boss, and I went to Myanmar and spent a couple of days there meeting with officials. It was tough. The reason was that not much progress had taken place there in twenty years. We did not expect it to be easy. I think the jury is still out as to whether we will achieve progress. There is much happy talk in the region about this. People are saying, "There is great progress. The United States and Myanmar are talking." It is perhaps useful that we are talking, but that is not progress. Progress will come when there is change on the ground in Myanmar. So far, there has been none. I just want to highlight that it is important to be careful and scrupulous in our analysis of the situation and not confuse process with progress. We certainly hope that there will be progress, as Kurt Campbell said several times in public. We knew that the going would be difficult. In the end, the question is whether there will be some moves out of Myanmar. It will be very important that our ASEAN colleagues work with us to encourage some steps. Even some small steps can be a start.

To sum up, the United States wants member countries to be successful in building the ASEAN Community. This is in our interest and works to our advantage too. An ASEAN with strong political, economic, and cultural bonds among its members will mean a more prosperous and more stable partner for the United States. We will demonstrate our commitment to ASEAN's success through increased and more intensive interaction at all levels, and by working together to confront the very real challenges in this region and the larger world community.

Note

1. Adapted from the remarks by Scot Marciel, Deputy Assistant Secretary of State of the United States and U.S. Ambassador for ASEAN Affairs, at the Institute of Southeast Asian Studies, Singapore, on 9 December 2009. His talk was a part of the ASEAN Studies Centre's ASEAN Ambassadors Seminar Series. Marciel is currently U.S. Ambassador to Indonesia.

7

MARITIME SECURITY IN SOUTHEAST ASIA AND THE UNITED STATES

Ian Storey

Southeast Asia is essentially a maritime region. All ten Association of Southeast Asian Nations (ASEAN) members bar one — Laos — depend on the sea for commerce and food security. Singapore is an island state, the Philippines and Indonesia are archipelagic countries, and Malaysia, Thailand, Myanmar, and Vietnam have extensive coastlines. Although Brunei and Cambodia have relatively short coastlines, the former relies on offshore hydrocarbon reserves to sustain its GDP growth, while the latter views potential oil and gas reserves in the Gulf of Thailand as an important contributor to its future economic growth. Southeast Asia's only non-ASEAN member, East Timor, is also fundamentally a maritime nation whose future economic health depends in large part on the exploitation of offshore energy reserves and fisheries.

It would be difficult to overstate the importance of Southeast Asia's maritime domain to the ASEAN states as well as to the wider global community. The multiple sea lines of communication

(SLOCs) which criss-cross and traverse the region, especially the South China Sea, link the Pacific and Indian Oceans and are of critical importance, not only to the coastal states of Southeast Asia, but also to trading nations around the world. More than 90 per cent of global trade is carried by sea, and Southeast Asian SLOCs are critical to the flow of much of this commerce. Maritime traffic traversing the South China Sea must also pass through one of the main choke points that provide access into and egress from, the South China Sea, notably the Malacca and Singapore Straits to the southwest, and the Luzon and Taiwan Straits to the northeast, as well as the Balabac Strait and waterways through the Philippines archipelago and the Sulu Sea to the east. The Strait of Malacca is particularly important as it provides the shortest route between the Indian Ocean and the South China Sea, and is used by more than 70,000 vessels every year carrying 15 million barrels of oil in 2006 and an estimated one third of world trade.[1] The Sunda and Lombok-Makassar Straits are also heavily used by ships transiting from the Indian Ocean to the Western Pacific, especially Very Large Crude Carriers. Southeast Asian SLOCs and choke points are thus critical to the energy security of Northeast Asia's economic powerhouses as they provide a crucial part of the route between key energy sources in the Middle East, Australia, and (increasingly) Africa and the energy-hungry economies of East Asia: the People's Republic of China (PRC), Taiwan, Japan, and South Korea are all dependent on uninterrupted energy supplies, largely in the form of oil, natural gas, and coal, much of which flows through the South China Sea. For example, more than 90 per cent of Japan's oil needs are imported. In 2006, China imported approximately 43 per cent of its energy needs, and by 2020, this dependency is predicted to rise to 60 per cent or higher.[2] In light of this, freedom of navigation and the safety of shipping through the South China Sea are of profound and increasing importance to countries in both Southeast and Northeast Asia.

In addition to the strategically important SLOCs, the seas of Southeast Asia are home to significant energy, mineral, and fishery resources. Brunei, Malaysia, Indonesia, Myanmar, and Vietnam are already significant players in the oil and gas industry, and as noted above, Cambodia and East Timor hope to join their ranks soon. Contested sovereignty claims in the South China Sea have been motivated in part by the widely held perception that the seabed holds significant reserves of energy deposits. Yet, estimates of the potential seabed energy reserves of the South China Sea vary significantly, though ongoing tensions have limited exploration work. Nonetheless, even if the South China Sea ultimately does not prove to be as hydrocarbons-rich as some currently suppose it to be, the "oil factor", that is, the perception that the South China Sea may be host to vast oil riches, remains a powerful driver of this regional dispute. Furthermore, the South China Sea hosts a fishery of global significance, accounting for 10 per cent of the landed catch,[3] and is consequently fundamental to the food security of coastal populations measured in the tens or even hundreds of millions.

The United States of America has had vital and enduring economic and strategic interests in maritime Southeast Asia since the end of World War II. Arguably the importance of these interests has substantially increased since the beginning of the twenty-first century for three reasons. First, the globalization of world trade has resulted in a phenomenal increase in the volume of seaborne trade: in 2007, 8.02 billion tons of goods were moved by sea, up from 6.27 billion in 2000 and 2.6 billion in 1970.[4] Second, the United States has focused on the need to address transnational security threats in the post–11 September 2001 (9/11) environment, including piracy/sea robbery, the potential for maritime terrorism, and the need to counter Weapons of Mass Destruction (WMD) proliferation. Third, the rise of China and the rapid modernization of the People's Liberation Army Navy (PLAN) have raised the prospect of a nascent Sino-U.S. naval rivalry which could be played out in the waters of Southeast Asia. The purpose of this chapter is to examine U.S. maritime security interests in Southeast Asia, specifically two issues: first, freedom of navigation and the free flow of maritime trade; and second, U.S. assistance to regional states to combat transnational threats at sea.

THE UNITED STATES AND FREEDOM OF NAVIGATION IN MARITIME SOUTHEAST ASIA

One of America's primary national interests in Southeast Asia is to uphold freedom of navigation at sea. Southeast Asia's sea lanes are not only of critical importance to the U.S. economy — and those of its friends and allies in the region — but they also allow the U.S. Navy to transit between the Indian and Pacific Oceans, greatly facilitating America's global military posture. As U.S. State Department Deputy Assistant Secretary Scot Marciel told the Congressional Committee on Foreign Affairs in July 2009, "The United States has long had a vital interest in maintaining stability, freedom of navigation, and the right to lawful commercial activity in East Asia's waterways. For decades, active U.S. engagement in East Asia, including the forward-deployed presence of U.S. forces[,] has been a central factor in keeping the peace and preserving those interests. That continues to be true today. Through diplomacy, commerce, and our military presence, we have protected vital U.S. interests."[5]

Since the end of the Cold War, the majority of Southeast Asian states have continued to support the U.S. military presence in the region as a stabilizing factor. Many ASEAN members have actively facilitated that presence by opening their ports to U.S. naval ship visits. This strategy, known as "places not bases", avoids the need for Southeast Asian countries to host permanent, and controversial, U.S. military facilities and bases. Singapore has been particularly supportive of U.S. naval operations in Southeast Asia. Following the closure of U.S. bases in the Philippines in 1992, Singapore agreed to host the U.S. Seventh Fleet's logistical support unit, Command Logistics Group Western Pacific (COMLOGWESTPAC), and in 2002 opened a pier at Changi Naval Base designed specifically to accommodate U.S. aircraft carriers. Today, Singapore receives more than 150 U.S. Navy ship visits per year. Ports in Malaysia, Thailand, Indonesia, Brunei, and the Philippines have also received U.S. ship visits on a regular basis, and, since the early 2000s, so has Vietnam.

As part of its forward-deployed presence, the U.S. Navy holds regular exercises with Southeast Asian navies. These exercises help build capacity, as well as increase interoperability. The U.S. Navy holds regular exercises with its counterparts from Singapore, Malaysia, Thailand, Indonesia, the Philippines, and Brunei. Foremost among these exercises is the annual bilateral Cooperation Afloat Readiness and Training (CARAT) exercise conducted with the above six countries since 1995 (in 2010, Cambodia participated in CARAT for the first time). Through exercises such as CARAT, the U.S. Navy has been able to build relationships with its regional counterparts that have proved invaluable in real world situations, such as relief operations in Aceh following the devastating tsunami on 26 December 2004.

As noted earlier, the South China Sea is Southeast Asia's most important body of water. Yet it is in the South China Sea that six parties — China, Taiwan, Vietnam, the Philippines, Malaysia, and Brunei — contest sovereignty over the Spratly Islands. Since 2007 tensions in the South China Sea have been on the upswing due to a combination of rising nationalism, increasing friction over access to energy and fishery resources, attempts by the disputants to bolster their respective jurisdictional claims, and the rapid modernization of the PLAN, which is shifting the military balance of power in China's favour.[6] Over the past few years, the United States has raised its concerns over developments in the South China Sea which could undermine freedom of navigation and impact the activities of U.S. companies in the area negatively.

The United States does not take a position on the competing claims of the six parties in the South China Sea. America's basic policy position is that freedom of navigation is sacrosanct, and that the dispute should be resolved peacefully, without recourse to force or the threat to use force, and in accordance with international law. In the 1990s, Washington noted with concern the growing instability in the South China Sea, and therefore welcomed the easing of tensions in the first half of this decade following the issuing of the ASEAN-China Declaration on the Conduct of Parties in the South China Sea (DoC) in 2002. As friction intensified after 2007, however, U.S. officials once again began to voice concern. Speaking at the 2008 Shangri-La Dialogue (SLD), for instance, U.S. Secretary of Defense Robert Gates underscored the security implications of rising demand for resources and the inherent dangers of "coercive diplomacy ... even when they coexist beside outward displays of cooperation".[7] While Gates did not explicitly identify China as the agent of this "coercive diplomacy", his comment was undoubtedly a clear reference to the controversy over British Petroleum's commercial activities in Vietnam, and was reinforced within a few months with the revelation that ExxonMobil had come under similar pressure from China to cease development projects off the Vietnamese coast.

Oblique criticism of China's greater assertiveness in the South China Sea gave way to a more forthright exposition of U.S. concerns in mid-2009, when two senior administration officials testified before the Senate Foreign Relations Committee on maritime disputes in East Asia. Scot Marciel confirmed that China had put foreign energy companies under pressure to suspend work on projects off the Vietnamese coast, that Washington objected to "any effort to intimidate U.S. companies", and had raised its concerns directly with Beijing.[8] In this context, Marciel noted that then Deputy Secretary of State John Negroponte had travelled to Hanoi in September 2008, a few months after the ExxonMobil story had broke, to assert the rights of U.S. companies operating in the South China Sea, a visit that went largely unnoticed by the media. Marciel went on to point out that the ambiguous nature of China's jurisdictional claims in the South China Sea had become of greater concern to Washington, because the areas in which Beijing had warned U.S. energy companies not to operate seemed to lie outside China's claimed maritime boundaries. He therefore called on the Chinese Government to provide greater clarity on the substance of its claims.

In his testimony, Deputy Assistant Secretary of Defense Robert Scher remarked that while the United States supported a negotiated settlement to the dispute, rising tensions over the past few years had prompted the Pentagon to reinforce measures designed to enhance stability in the area. This strategy consists of an enhanced U.S. military presence in the region, including operations by the U.S. Navy in the South China Sea to assert freedom of navigation rights, and the expansion and deepening of defence diplomacy and capacity building programmes with regional states such as Malaysia, Vietnam, the Philippines, and Indonesia "to prevent tensions in the South China Sea from developing into a threat to US interests". With regard to the last point, Scher pointed out that U.S.-led security cooperation activities, such as regular exercises identified earlier in this chapter, helped regional states "overcome longstanding historical and cultural barriers that inhibit multilateral cooperation".[9] In short, America's military presence in Southeast Asia helps provide a stable environment for the claimants to pursue a political solution and encourages the ASEAN states to increase defence cooperation among themselves at the same time.

U.S. concerns were highlighted again at the 2010 SLD by Defense Secretary Gates who described the South China Sea dispute as an "area of growing concern for the United States". He reiterated long-standing U.S. policy — that America has a vital interest in the maintenance of stability and freedom of navigation in the sea, does not take sides on competing sovereignty claims, and opposes the use of force to resolve the problem. But he added that the United States objected "to any effort to intimidate US corporations or those of any other nation engaged in legitimate economic activity", a clear reference to attempts by China to pressure foreign energy corporations — including U.S. giant ExxonMobil — into suspending oil and gas projects in disputed waters off the Vietnamese coast.

Gates' comments on the South China Sea should be considered in conjunction with recent statements made by senior U.S. military officers regarding the impact of China's military modernization on the dispute. In congressional testimony in January 2010, Pacific Command (PACOM) Commander Admiral Robert Willard suggested that China's "aggressive program of military modernization" appeared designed to "challenge U.S. freedom of action in the region and, if necessary, enforce China's influence over its neighbors — including our regional allies and partners".[10] In a speech to the Asia Society in Washington DC on 9 June 2010, Admiral Mike Mullins, chairman of the Joint Chiefs of Staff, expressed "genuine concern" at China's military build-up which, he argued, seems "oddly out of step with their stated goal of territorial defense".[11] A week later, Admiral Patrick Walsh, commander of the U.S. Pacific Fleet, told a Japanese newspaper that the United States was concerned that Chinese assertiveness in the South China Sea risked endangering freedom of navigation and the flow of maritime trade.[12]

Increased American focus on the South China Sea has also been animated by China's increased military capabilities in the area, particularly at Sanya on Hainan Island. The Yulin Naval Base, construction of which began in the early 2000s, is now home to advanced power projection assets, such as nuclear submarines and surface combatants, and will likely be the home port for China's future aircraft carriers.[13] The build-up of naval forces at Sanya has led the United States to increase surveillance of the PLAN in the South China Sea, a development that the Chinese Government considers provocative and illegal. A number of confrontations between the United States and Chinese vessels took place in early 2009, culminating in the standoff between the survey vessel *USNS Impeccable* and five Chinese-flagged vessels, seventy-five miles off Hainan Island in March.[14] This was followed a few months later by an incident in which a Chinese submarine damaged a U.S. destroyer's towed array sonar in international waters off Subic

Bay in the Philippines.[15] In reference to the *Impeccable* incident in his congressional testimony in July 2009, Marciel described China's actions as inimical to freedom of navigation and part of a pattern of growing assertiveness by China over its perceived maritime rights. Both Marciel and Scher called for dialogue between the two sides to strengthen communications and reduce the risk of further incidents at sea. To that end, in August 2009, American and Chinese officials held a special session under the 1998 Military Maritime Consultative Agreement, but little progress was made. Chinese officials at the meeting reportedly reiterated their country's legal right to restrict foreign military activities in their Exclusive Economic Zone (EEZ) and called on the United States to end its surveillance activities off China's coast.[16] Although the two sides agreed to continue discussions, given their differing interpretations of international maritime law, and the build-up of military forces in the area, incidents such as those involving the *Impeccable* could well become more frequent.

THE UNITED STATES AND MARITIME TRANSNATIONAL SECURITY THREATS

The 9/11 incident led Washington to consider potential threats to U.S. security in and from the maritime domain. In Southeast Asia, the United States has focused on two main security threats: first, the transit of WMDs through Southeast Asian ports and waters; second, maritime terrorism, the problem of so-called "ungoverned spaces", and the possible nexus between terrorism and piracy. Since 9/11 the United States has proposed and operationalized a number of security initiatives to address these threats in partnership with Southeast Asian countries. However, while ASEAN members have been broadly receptive to U.S. security concerns in the region, few of Washington's initiatives have been free of controversy.

U.S. counter-WMD proliferation efforts in Southeast Asia have centred on the Container Security Initiative (CSI) and Proliferation

Security Initiative (PSI). CSI was proposed in 2002 as a means for the United States and partner countries to identify high-risk cargo in containers before they are loaded on to ships bound for the United States. The primary concern was that transnational terrorist groups such as al-Qaeda might place radioactive material and explosives — a so-called "dirty bomb" — inside a container which would then be set off in U.S. territory. A series of agreements was signed between the United States and other countries which allowed for the pre-screening of containers for radiological material before being shipped to the United States. Since 2002, fifty-eight foreign ports have participated in CSI, accounting for 85 per cent of container traffic bound for America. In Southeast Asia, CSI operates in four major ports: Singapore (2003), Laem Chabang in Thailand (2004), and Port Klang and Tanjung Pelepas in Malaysia (2004). Subsequently, in 2007, Singapore became one of six international ports to participate in the Secure Freight Initiative (SFI), which enhanced scanning of containers for radiation.

In May 2003 the United States unveiled PSI. The initiative aims to forge a coalition of like-minded countries to cooperate to interdict chemical, biological, or nuclear-weapon technology and capabilities at sea (or in the air) to and from states and non-state actors of proliferation concern. PSI also seeks to streamline procedures for the rapid exchange of relevant information concerning WMD proliferation. PSI proved to be more controversial than CSI in that a number of countries questioned its legitimacy under international law, particularly its intent to stop and search ships on the high seas. In Southeast Asia only Singapore — which is a close security partner of the United States and also describes itself as an "iconic target" for transnational terrorist groups — formally signed up to PSI. Since joining in 2004, Singapore has hosted two major PSI multinational interdiction exercises: Deep Sabre I in 2005 and Deep Sabre II in 2009. According to the U.S. State Department, Brunei, Cambodia, and the Philippines also participate in PSI although they have not taken part in multilateral exercises.[17]

In 2004 the United States began to express increasing disquiet over the rise of piracy and sea robbery attacks in Southeast Asia, and the potential for transnational terrorist groups to conduct an attack in maritime domains. The two most commonly cited scenarios included terrorists sinking one or more large vessels in the Strait of Malacca in an attempt to block the waterway and disrupt the world economy, and militants using a crude oil or natural gas tanker as a "floating bomb" in a major Asian port.

Southeast Asia is no stranger to acts of maritime terrorism. In the Philippines, the radical Abu Sayyaf Group (ASG) has been active in the maritime domain since it was formed in the early 1990s, and in February 2004 the group committed the world's worst act of maritime terrorism to date by sinking SuperFerry 14 in Manila Bay with the loss of 116 lives. In December 2001 Singapore's security services arrested thirteen members of al-Qaeda-linked Jemaah Islamiyah (JI) whose plans included suicide attacks against visiting U.S. naval vessels using high-speed boats packed with explosives.[18]

The threat of maritime terrorism in Southeast Asia may well have been overstated, especially in the Malacca Strait. Nonetheless, it was a threat that could not be ruled out. In testimony before the U.S. Congress on 31 March 2004, Admiral Thomas Fargo, commander of the U.S. military's largest combatant command, PACOM, based in Honolulu, Hawaii, unveiled a new programme designed to increase cooperation between the United States and Southeast Asian countries to address transnational security threats at sea, including terrorism, piracy, proliferation of WMDs, and illegal trafficking — the Regional Maritime Security Initiative (RMSI).[19]

During his testimony, Fargo stated that in operational terms, PACOM was considering "putting Special Operations Forces on high-speed vessels" to conduct effective interdiction. But press reports in Indonesia erroneously claimed that PACOM intended to station Special Operations Forces in the Strait of Malacca to deal with rising piracy attacks. The Malaysian and Indonesian Governments bristled at the reports, condemning the proposal as a violation of their sovereignty and warned that the presence of U.S. forces in the strait would only fuel Islamic radicalism in Southeast Asia.[20] Singapore, dependent for its prosperity on the unimpeded flow of maritime trade and perceiving itself as a target by groups such as JI and al-Qaeda, took the threat of maritime terrorism much more seriously than Kuala Lumpur or Jakarta, and offered tacit support for RMSI.[21]

It was left to then U.S. Defense Secretary Donald Rumsfeld in June 2004 to soothe Indonesian and Malaysian ire by stating that it was never America's intention to station military forces in the Malacca Strait permanently. The damage to RMSI, however, could not be undone, and PACOM ceased using the acronym; though, as described below, the programme's intent survived. Nonetheless, by rejecting RMSI, the ball was now firmly in the court of the three littoral states, Indonesia, Malaysia, and Singapore. Reacting to international pressure, the three countries launched coordinated naval patrols in the Strait of Malacca in 2004, and in 2005 added combined aerial patrols. The Malacca Strait Patrols (MSP), together with a series of national initiatives to improve maritime security, paid strong dividends. The International Maritime Bureau's Piracy Reporting Centre in Kuala Lumpur has recorded a significant downward trend in the number of recorded incidents of piracy and sea robbery in Southeast Asia: the number of reported attacks fell from 187 in 2003 to forty-five in 2009. Incidents of maritime depredations in the Strait of Malacca declined from thirty-eight in 2004 to just two in 2009. Particularly striking has been the improvement in Indonesian waters; down from a high of 121 attacks in 2003 to fifteen in 2009.[22] The United States has commended the security cooperation among the littoral states. In 2006 then U.S. Chief of Naval Operations Admiral Michael Mullins declared that the MSP had had a "big impact" on the level of maritime crime in Southeast Asia, while PACOM Commander Admiral Timothy Keating noted that security in the Strait of Malacca is "much different and much improved in just the last five years".[23]

The United States has played an important role in helping Southeast Asian states address transnational threats at sea, including piracy and sea robbery. Although the 2004 controversy turned RMSI into a toxic acronym, the aim of assisting Southeast Asian countries to improve maritime surveillance and interdiction capabilities was given significant financial backing by the Bush administration. These financial resources have been used to help Indonesia and Malaysia improve security in the Strait of Malacca, but because the MSP and other initiatives have mitigated that problem, the United States redirected its efforts towards improving security in the so-called triborder sea area, an area encompassing the Sulu Sea in the southwestern Philippines and off Sabah province in eastern Malaysia, and the Celebes Sea which is enclosed by Sabah, the Sulu archipelago, and Mindanao in the southern Philippines, and Indonesia's Sulawesi Island. Over the years, the triborder area has gained a notorious reputation for illegal maritime activities such as piracy, smuggling, and illegal trafficking, and, more seriously, as a transit route for ASG and JI members to move between the southern Philippines, Sabah, and Indonesia. Neglected for decades by the governments of Jakarta and Manila, the triborder area has been characterized by some analysts as an "ungoverned space" and "theatre of jihadi operations".[24]

Concerned about the dangers posed by such ungoverned spaces, Section 1206 of the U.S. National Defense Authorization Act for Fiscal Year 2006 (FY06) authorized the Department of Defense (DoD) to assist foreign countries build and sustain military forces capable of conducting counterterrorism operations. Section 1206 funding allows PACOM to concentrate on maritime, riverine, border, and port security efforts, and so far the geographic focus has been on the triborder sea area, as well as the Malacca Strait and parts of South Asia. Southeast Asian maritime states, particularly Indonesia, Malaysia, and the Philippines, have been among the biggest recipients of Section 1206 funds, also known as the Global Train and Equip Program. Between 2006 and 2009 the United

States provided Indonesia with US$56 million worth of equipment to enhance maritime security, including five coastal surveillance radars installed along the Indonesian side of the Strait of Malacca, and seven in the Makassar Strait and Celebes Sea.[25] The Integrated Maritime Surveillance System for Indonesia covers more than 1,205 kilometres in the Straits of Malacca and 1,285 kilometres of coastline in the Sulu and Celebes seas.[26] During the same period, Malaysia received US$43 million in U.S. assistance, including US$2.2 million to enhance its aerial surveillance capabilities, and US$13.6 million for nine coastal surveillance radars along the coast of Sabah. The Philippines received US$31 million to upgrade the maritime surveillance and interdiction capabilities of the Philippines Armed Forces.[27] According to one agency, the Global Train and Equip Program is considered DoD's "single most important tool to shape the environment and counter terrorism outside Iraq and Afghanistan".[28] Unlike the ill-fated RMSI proposal, equipment under Section 1206 authorization has been provided to Southeast Asian countries with minimal publicity. In addition to Global Train and Equip, the United States has also been providing capacity building support to Southeast Asian navies through the annual Southeast Asia Cooperation against Terrorism (SEACAT). The United States Coast Guard (USCG) has also conducted training programmes for the various maritime law enforcement agencies in Southeast Asia.

Notes

1. Marine Department Malaysia website <http://www.marine.gov.my/service/index.html>; U.S. Energy Information Administration (2005) and World Oil Transit Chokepoints website <http://www.eia.doe.gov/cabs/World_Oil_Transit_Chokepoints/Malacca.html>. When local, cross-strait traffic is included, this figure rises considerably to exceed 90,000 vessels of larger than 100 gross registered tons. See, S. Bateman, J.H. Ho, and M. Mathai, "Shipping Patterns in the Straits of Malacca and Singapore: An Assessment of the Risks to Different Types of Vessel", *Contemporary Southeast Asia* 29, no. 2 (2007): 309–32.
2. "China's Dependence on Imported Oil Increases", *China Daily*, 22 June 2007.
3. See UNEP/GEF Reversing Environmental Degradation Trends in the South China Sea and Gulf of Thailand project website <www.unepscs.org.>

4. United Nations Conference on Trade and Development (UNCTAD), *Review of Maritime Transport 2008* (New York and Geneva: United Nations, 2008), p. xiii.

5. Testimony of Deputy Assistant Secretary Scot Marciel, Bureau of East Asian and Pacific Affairs, U.S. Department of State, before the Subcommittee on East Asian and Pacific Affairs, Committee on Foreign Relations, United States Senate, 15 July 2009 <http://foreign.senate.gov/testimony/2009/MarcielTestimony090715p.pdf.> (accessed 15 July 2010).

6. Clive Schofield and Ian Storey, "The South China Sea Dispute: Increasing Stakes and Rising Tensions", Jamestown Foundation Occasional Paper, November 2009.

7. International Institute for Strategic Studies (Singapore), speech as delivered by Secretary of Defense Robert M. Gates, Singapore, 31 May 2008 <http://www.defenselink.mil/speeches/speech.aspx?speechid=1253> (accessed 15 July 2010).

8. Testimony of Deputy Assistant Secretary Scot Marciel.

9. Testimony of Deputy Assistant Secretary of Defense Robert Scher, Asian and Pacific Security Affairs, Office of the Secretary of Defense, before the Subcommittee on East Asian and Pacific Affairs, Committee on Foreign Relations, United States Senate, 15 July 2009 <http://foreign.senate.gov/testimony/2009/ScherTestimony090715p.pdf> (accessed 15 July 2010).

10. Statement of Admiral Robert F. Willard, United States Navy, Commander, United States Pacific Command, before the House Armed Services Committee on Recent Security Developments Involving China, 13 January 2010.

11. Admiral Mullen's speech at the 2010 Asia Society Washington's Annual Dinner <http://www.asiasociety.org/policy-politics/international-relations/us-asia/adm-mullens-speech-2010-asia-society-washingtons-ann?page=0%2C3> (accessed 15 July 2010).

12. "U.S. Commander Blasts Chinese Navy's Behaviour", *Asahi Shimbun*, 15 June 2010.

13. See, Richard D. Fisher Jr., "Secret Sanya — China's New Nuclear Naval Base Revealed", *Jane's Intelligence Review,* April 2008.

14. See, Ian Storey, "Impeccable Affair and Renewed Rivalry in the South China Sea", *China Brief* 9, no. 9 (30 April 2009).

15. "China Ship Hits U.S. Sonar", *Straits Times*, 13 June 2009.

16. "End Military Surveillance Missions, China Tells U.S." Associated Press, 28 August 2009.

17. See <http://www.state.gov/t/isn/c27732.htm>.

18. For a complete account see *The Jemaah Islamiyah Arrests and the Threat of Terrorism* (Singapore: Ministry of Home Affairs, January 2003).

19. Testimony of Admiral Thomas B. Fargo, United States Navy, Commander, U.S. Pacific Command, before the House Armed Services Committee, U.S. House of Representatives, regarding U.S. Pacific Command Posture, 31 March 2004 <http://pacom.mil/speeches/sst2004/040331housearmedsvcscomm.shtml> (accessed 15 July 2010).

20. "Singapore Can't Invite U.S. to Patrol Straits: KL", *Straits Times*, 12 May 2004.

21. Keynote address by Minister for Defence Rear Admiral (RADM) (NS) Teo Chee Hean at the opening of the 2nd Western Pacific MCMEX and DIVEX, 26 April 2004 <http://www.mindef.gov.sg/display.asp?number=2073.> (accessed 15 July 2010).

22. See IMB, *Piracy and Armed Robbery against Ships: Annual Report 1 January–31 December 2009*, January 2010.

23. "U.S. Navy Leaders Laud Southeast Asian Anti-Piracy Steps", *Jakarta Post*, 4 November 2006, and "Official: Malacca Strait Security Better", Associated Press, 16 April 2007.

24. Angel Rabasa et al., *Ungoverned Territories: Understanding and Reducing Terrorism Risks* (Santa Monica, CA: RAND Corporation, 2007), p. 116.

25. Information provided to the author by the U.S. Embassy in Jakarta, May 2009.

26. "U.S. Envoy Dedicates Maritime Radar Equipment for Indonesia", Antara News, 30 June 2010.

27. Nina M. Serafino, "Section 1206 of the National Defense Authorization Act for FY2006: A Fact Sheet on Department of Defense Authority to Train and Equip Foreign Military Forces", *Congressional Research Service Report for Congress*, 15 May 2008 <http://ftp.fas.org/sgp/crs/natsec/RS22855.pdf> (accessed 15 July 2010).

28. See Fiscal Year 2009 Budget Estimates, Defense Security Cooperation Agency, February 2008 <http://www.defenselink.mil/comptroller/defbudget/fy2009/budget_justification/pdfs/01_Operation_and_Maintenance/O_M_VOL_1_PARTS/DSCA%20FY%2009%20PB%20OP-5.pdf> (accessed 15 July 2010).

8

ASEAN'S VIEWS ON THE U.S. MILITARY ROLE IN THE REGION[1]

Collin S.L. Koh

Southeast Asia, being strategically positioned in the region, stands at the confluence of great power rivalry and, at the same time, faces a multitude of non-traditional security challenges as well as residual intramural rivalries. The Barack Obama administration on its part adopts a moderate, fiscally-sustainable security approach and is regarded to continue roughly similar military involvement in Southeast Asia. Obama's policy also stresses multilateral cooperation and, in this regard, burden sharing. This is a welcome policy stance, but one that is also a cause for concern over the possible decline of the United States and its reduced commitment towards regional security. These concerns are largely unfounded. It is apparent that U.S. military commitments to the Asia-Pacific on the whole will remain consistent. This is illustrated in the professed intent by Washington to augment the U.S. Navy Seventh Fleet — the linchpin of American military power in the region — in apparent response to China's military rise and increased assertiveness, Korean Peninsula problems, and emerging non-traditional security (NTS) risks.

The basic foundations of the U.S. military role in Southeast Asia remain largely unchanged from the ones that existed under the Bush administration. However, U.S. military involvement may increasingly become issue focused, especially with regard to NTS risks. The Obama administration is focusing on NTS as the basis of sustainable military cooperation with ASEAN. This bodes well for capacity-constrained ASEAN. In the face of geopolitical uncertainties, ASEAN countries from the time of the Bush administration have been attempting to build up their own defence and security capacities. Intraregional defence and security cooperation also appear to have hastened, as seen in talks about the pooling together of national-level military capacities, primarily targeted at NTS issues, and ideas about formal military cooperation.

Other than intensifying efforts in regional security cooperation, ASEAN continues to adopt a "business as usual" hedging approach, particularly in the accumulation of national military capacities, especially force-projection assets. The inherent risk is that these capabilities might pose a classic security dilemma, especially given the outstanding territorial disagreements in the region. To sustain U.S.-ASEAN military relations, the United States should continue to fill niche roles by leveraging its power-projection capabilities, especially in NTS contingencies. At the same time, it should encourage ASEAN to maintain non-provocative defence postures, allowing for sufficient deterrent and response capacity against NTS threats, while at the same time mitigating the prospects of a security dilemma.

SETTING THE STAGE

The November 2008 election of President Barack Obama appeared to foreshadow a new era in the United States' Asia-Pacific security policy. One of the most notable aspects has been the increased interest evinced by the Obama administration to engage Southeast Asia. This has all been happening against the backdrop of an ever changing, unpredictable security landscape in the Asia-Pacific (including Southeast Asia), which warrants necessary adjustments of the U.S. military role in the region. Without doubt, the United States possesses the most powerful military capability in the Asia-Pacific and this position, notwithstanding the emergence of potential competitors, will remain viable and continue to give Washington considerable leverage in shaping the regional security environment. Therefore, it is important to examine the prospects of future U.S. military roles in the region with respect to ASEAN — a regional organization which has significant influence on the implementation of Washington's security policy in the broader Asia-Pacific. This is precisely what this chapter strives to accomplish. First, it shall briefly illuminate the contemporary security developments in the Asia-Pacific and the role of Southeast Asia in the whole equation. Then, it compares the role of the U.S. military in Southeast Asia under the Bush and Obama administrations, and ASEAN policy responses. Finally, their implications are discussed and some policy recommendations presented as the way forward for a sustainable U.S.-ASEAN military relationship. This chapter argues that the approach taken by the Obama administration, which underpins basic U.S. military commitments in Southeast Asia, is welcomed by ASEAN, but the regional grouping to date has maintained a "business as usual" stance and continues to beef up its capacities.

ASEAN AND THE EVOLVING ASIA-PACIFIC SECURITY LANDSCAPE

The maritime geography of Southeast Asia presents a somewhat awkward paradigm for ASEAN and its ten member states. On the one hand, it endows the region with one of the primary bases of wealth and prosperity, given the importance of global maritime commerce, not to mention the rich marine resources residing in the region. On the other hand, this exposes ASEAN to a complex array of security challenges. This means that ASEAN states can barely afford to overlook whatever happens in and around Southeast Asia. The external and internal challenges are manifold. For ease of discussion, these challenges will be segregated into the conventional "traditional" and "non-traditional" (henceforth termed non-traditional security or NTS) aspects. These issues certainly warrant a more in-depth discussion in a chapter exclusively tailored for that. In this section, they are given a brief and simpler treatment.

Traditional Security Aspects: A Persistent Concern

With the end of the Cold War, superpower confrontation marked by the dire prospects of nuclear annihilation came to an end. While the "Peace Dividend" has taken hold in the post–Cold War euphoria that swept the western hemisphere, as seen in the rapid drawdown of military capabilities, the same is not happening in the eastern hemisphere. In the Asia-Pacific, the cloud of uncertainty has been the driving force behind frantic attempts at building up national military capabilities as a hedge against the emergence of regional hegemons – Japan and China being perceived as such back in the early nineties. The United States, on its part, remains engaged in the Asia-Pacific and has contributed towards an environment conducive to national development by regional states. The prospect of major war is considered remote, although low-intensity armed confrontations remain plausible, given the outstanding territorial disputes in the East and South China Seas, not to mention the Taiwan Strait and the Korean Peninsula, where the prospect of full-scale war remains likely if not properly managed. To date, these issues remain salient for ASEAN. In particular, ASEAN has to confront the reality of emerging great powers in the region. This development is not necessarily bad for ASEAN, considering it can benefit from the economic rise of China and India. However, the future remains uncertain from the security point of view. As a group of small and middle powers, ASEAN is strategically located on the Western Pacific rim, surrounded by these powerful rivalries which could have potentially drastic effects. The ASEAN states can only choose to ignore them at their own peril.

Non-Traditional Security (NTS) Aspects: An Ever-growing Concern

The Asia-Pacific represents one of the key growth regions of the world. However, it is also vulnerable to a range of NTS risks that can derail its continued development. The Asia-Pacific confronts a menagerie of challenges — non-state threats such as terrorism, climate change, and energy, food, and water shortages — all in the midst of ever rising population growth. First of all, Southeast Asia is particularly vulnerable to the effects of climate change, primarily sea level rise, a phenomenon which threatens to inundate coastal communities, particularly in archipelagic Indonesia and the Philippines.[2] The massive displacement of populations and the resultant refugee flows may have a negative transnational security impact on Southeast Asia. The Indian Ocean tsunami in December 2004, which ravaged coastal communities in some parts of the region, is indicative of the dangers relating to natural disasters. The vital sea lines of communication (SLOCs) through the waters of Southeast Asia are crucial arteries for the continued socio-economic development of the Asia-Pacific, particularly for China, Japan, and South Korea, all of which are dependent on energy imports from the Middle East. The interrelated nature of NTS risks means that regional governments face the daunting task of mitigating the consequent impact. ASEAN states have limited capacity in dealing with these security risks through unilateral measures alone. They can band together, depend on international institutions, or rely on some form of security guarantee from external parties. In the case of ASEAN, the United States fits this last role.

THE ROLE OF THE U.S. MILITARY IN SOUTHEAST ASIA: FROM BUSH TO OBAMA

For decades, the United States has been perceived as the predominant security player in the Asia-Pacific. Relations among most of the countries in the region have been characterized by a degree of distrust and mutual suspicion. Generally, these states rely on the United States to provide the needed security to pursue their national objectives. As Robert Sutter pointed out, these countries also recognize that rising regional powers do not necessarily desire to share the American burden, which is costly and involves great risk for preserving regional security.[3] As such, in the absence of willing partners to help maintain regional stability, the United States remains the sole security guarantor for the Asia-Pacific. However, the reality is that U.S. security focus in the region is not uniform to begin with.

One needs no reminder that the Asia-Pacific is made up of a variety of nations, all with diverse sets of constraints and vulnerabilities. U.S. security concerns in Southeast Asia have for most of the time been overshadowed by those in Northeast Asia, where flash points in the Taiwan Strait and Korean Peninsula attract the bulk of U.S. military attention. Some scholars, such as Alice Ba, attribute this lack of American attention to Southeast Asia to the fact that the latter has been relatively prosperous and stable compared with other, more volatile regions (such as the Middle East), and to the lack of cultural and geographical affinity between Southeast Asia and the United States, compared with Latin America, for example.[4] This American policy neglect of Southeast Asia took a twist in the aftermath of the 9/11 terror attacks.

The Bush Administration and ASEAN Perspectives

The Bush administration took an interest in furthering security links with Southeast Asia. One of the approaches was the cultivation of potential new partnerships, especially with Indonesia and Vietnam.[5]

Southeast Asia was then labelled as the "second front" in the "Global War on Terror" (GWOT), particularly after the terror bombings in Bali (2002) and Jakarta (2003). While not all that attention has been welcomed in Southeast Asia, GWOT represented a "modest renaissance" in U.S. security relations with the region, manifested in increased intelligence collaboration, new economic and military assistance, and expanded bilateral military links with some individual Southeast Asian states.[6] American military involvement in Southeast Asia, in the name of counterterrorism, according to some critics, was also a cover for an ulterior geopolitical motive: to counter the rising influence of China in the region.[7] The *2001 Quadrennial Defense Review* (QDR), emphasized the need to continue honouring international commitments, including the preclusion of hostile domination of critical areas.[8] This meant that, while the United States was concerned with waging GWOT in Southeast Asia, its traditional security concern remained. The *2006 QDR* specifically identified China among the major and emerging powers as having the greatest potential to compete militarily with the United States.[9] However, compared with the *2001 QDR*, the 2006 document stressed the need for U.S. forces to operate globally.[10] The *2001 QDR* pointed to the need to rely more on assets capable of sustained operations at great distances, with minimal theatre-based support.[11] Thus, Washington endeavoured to forge closer military links with Southeast Asia, but appeared to have recognized the difficulty of securing additional access to facilities.[12] The notable exception was the U.S.-Singapore agreement on the use of the Changi Naval Base, an issue which provoked an outcry from the island city state's larger neighbours. Apparently noting the sensitivities involved, Washington, on signing a U.S.-ASEAN counterterrorism pact in 2002, reassured ASEAN states that it had no intention of stationing ground troops in the region, outside the U.S.-Philippine Visiting Forces Agreement, which allowed for some 1,500 U.S. troops in the southern Philippines.[13] This was a welcome statement, since the stationing of U.S. forces in Southeast Asia could potentially inflame religious extremism and nationalism. ASEAN appeared receptive to the counterterrorism pact upon Washington's reassurance. Malaysia's Foreign Minister Syed Hamid Albar, for instance, remarked that this was not a case of "Big Brother United States" imposing on ASEAN.[14]

However, the general GWOT approach adopted by the Bush administration was regarded as unilateralist and sparked anti-Western sentiments among the Muslim populace in Southeast Asia, thus causing significant concerns among the Muslim ASEAN governments in particular.[15] In the 2002 *National Security Strategy of the United States of America* report, the Bush administration emphasized the need to "act pre-emptively" to forestall or prevent hostile acts.[16] This brought about a whole new problem for some ASEAN countries, this time not about the stationing of troops in the region, but about the likelihood of U.S. military forces conducting surprise, surgical operations against perceived terrorist targets on their soil without prior consent. This was compounded by the fact that, not desiring to be restricted in its freedom of action, the Bush administration refused to accede to ASEAN's Treaty of Amity and Cooperation (TAC).[17] Shortly after an official U.S. statement in 2002 was issued, which suggested the idea of conducting surprise attacks on suspected terrorist targets in Southeast Asia, Kuala Lumpur warned that any covert U.S. military action against terrorist targets, such as the controversial missile strike led by the Central Intelligence Agency in Yemen, would be unacceptable in the region. The then Defence Minister (now Prime Minister) of Malaysia, Najib Tun Razak, remarked, "We do not need any foreign interference or foreign troops in the country. We are capable of fighting terrorists."[18] ASEAN states had reacted cautiously to U.S. efforts to bolster military ties with the region, especially with respect to any direct U.S. role in suppressing local militant threats. Due to this political sensitivity, especially for governments of Muslim ASEAN states, and the need to take into account the interest of domestic constituencies, the ASEAN states preferred a rather low profile for the U.S. military role in the region. In 2006, during a visit to Jakarta to discuss closer bilateral military cooperation, U.S. Defense Secretary Donald Rumsfeld was bluntly reminded by his Indonesian counterpart that an overbearing U.S. approach in counterterrorism had led many in the world to view U.S. power as a "threat".[19] Such ASEAN sentiments were displayed in the maritime security realm. In 2004, Washington suggested the idea of stationing military forces in the Strait of Malacca to fight terrorism under the rubric of the Regional Maritime Security Initiative.[20] Despite perceptual differences among the concerned ASEAN littoral states, the eventual decision was made to exclude U.S. intervention in the congested waterways.[21] Indonesia, Malaysia, Singapore, and later, Thailand, combined efforts under the Malacca Strait Patrol initiative to secure the straits.

Perhaps the most important factor that continues to make the U.S. military presence in Southeast Asia appealing to ASEAN leaders is China; especially the latter's rapid military build-up. As Satu Limaye has pointed out, the very rise of China has led a number of Southeast Asian countries to seize the opportunity to enhance military relations with Washington.[22] The commander of the U.S. Pacific Command (PACOM), Admiral Timothy Keating, remarked in 2008 that the United States had to be ready for any possibilities until China clarified which direction it would take with its military power, adding that "until we are more certain about that, we must be ready to respond using all military options".[23] The U.S. Navy (USN) Seventh Fleet, based in Yokosuka, Japan, remains the linchpin of U.S. military power against emerging, potential hostile contenders in the region. The Bush administration apparently placed sufficient attention on maintaining the Seventh Fleet's combat capability, a commitment which is continued by the Obama administration. Southeast Asia features prominently in the Seventh Fleet's scope of operations. In particular, to bolster force interoperability and security in Southeast Asia, the Seventh Fleet continues to participate in bilateral and multinational exercises with regional navies; most notably in the annual Cooperation Afloat Readiness and Training (CARAT) and Southeast Asia Cooperation against Terrorism (SEACAT) drills.[24] The apparent shift in U.S. military focus to the Pacific can also be observed in the U.S. Air Force decision to procure a long-endurance multirole transport aircraft capable of rapid trans–Pacific Ocean deployments. Although limited in overall fleet size, the USN is transferring the bulk of its existing and planned forces to the Pacific. The U.S. Army and Marines have also restationed personnel and pre-positioned forces throughout the region, including a major base in Guam.[25] For all these measures taken by Washington, ASEAN leaders can be well assured of continued U.S. commitment to forestalling any negative consequences stemming from the military rise of China.

The Obama Administration and ASEAN Perspectives

It has been observed that the establishment of the Obama administration has been a great relief to many ASEAN countries, which view this as an opportunity for Washington to become re-engaged in Southeast Asia in light of the U.S. preoccupation elsewhere, especially in Afghanistan and Iraq. A notable act taken by the Obama administration has been the signing of the TAC with ASEAN. While some ASEAN states have reservations, the general sentiment has been pleasant on the whole.[26] Manila, for instance, remarked that the U.S. signing of the TAC "means that they (Washington) will get engaged with all the issues pertaining not only to ASEAN but to northeast Asia and Asia. The United States wants to get engaged and therefore it is good."[27] It appears that U.S. military commitments to Southeast Asia have not changed much, and probably are not going to, since the passing of the Bush era. The Obama administration's Asia-Pacific policy, according to Sutter, will be partly characterized by enhanced activism, involvement, and flexibility in Southeast Asia.[28] However, unlike its predecessor, the Obama administration takes on a more moderate approach towards security issues. Notably, in a sign of distancing itself from the Bush administration's unilateralist stance and being aware that the country's fiscal woes presented a long-term threat to its diplomatic clout, the Obama administration unveiled a new, fiscally sustainable national security doctrine in May 2010, stressing diplomatic engagement and economic discipline to augment mere military power, in order to bolster the international standing of the United States.[29] Calls to emphasize diplomacy over military power, however, did not mean a reversal of traditional commitments to preserving U.S. conventional military superiority, even if U.S. military forces are already overstretched.

The Asia-Pacific will become even more important to the U.S. defence and economic interests in the future, according to Admiral Keating.[30] With respect to new directions for U.S. military roles in the Asia-Pacific, the *2010 QDR* emphasized, among other things, the continual augmentation of regional deterrence and rapid response capabilities in the Asia-Pacific, while seeking opportunities to build the capacity of regional partners to respond more effectively to contingencies, including humanitarian crises and natural disasters. Like the previous *QDRs*, the 2010 document stresses the constraints that the U.S. military faces from vast geographical distances that characterize the Asia-Pacific, as well as the low density of U.S. basing and infrastructure. This necessitates seeking opportunities for a more forward-deployed presence that supports increased multilateral cooperation on maritime security, and enhanced capabilities for assured access to the sea, air, space, and cyberspace.[31] With respect to Southeast Asia, the *2010 QDR* not only mentions the continued enhancement of long-standing alliances and partnerships in the region, but also stresses the development of new strategic relationships with Indonesia, Malaysia, and Vietnam to address NTS risks. The continued development of multilateral institutions and other integrated approaches to regional security affairs is also encouraged.[32] Assistant Secretary of Defense for Asian and Pacific Security Affairs Wallace Gregson remarked that NTS issues need to be seriously considered when crafting a new strategy for the Asia-Pacific.[33] According to U.S. Department of

State officials, disaster risk management may become the basis of a new model of U.S. engagement in Southeast Asia, building on the success of such cooperation between Manila and Washington.[34] If so, this testifies to an issue-focused approach adopted by the Obama administration when it comes to crafting a sustainable U.S. military role in the region, beyond the GWOT-focused predilection of the previous administration. Thus, it marks a noteworthy enhancement of the U.S.-ASEAN military links that existed before the Obama administration.

While the current Obama administration appears repeatedly to proclaim that the United States is back in Asia to stay, some commentators feel that the *2010 QDR* may fail to convince U.S. allies in the region that Washington will retain both the resolve and the capacity to maintain a decisive military edge in the region.[35] Asian governments are said to be nervous that the U.S. decline is real this time.[36] The view in Jakarta and other Asian capitals is that the Obama administration will maintain existing U.S. policies in the region for at least the next year or two, being bogged down by other, more pressing issues, such as Afghanistan and Iraq, besides having to deal with the global financial crisis and a battered U.S. economy.[37] Within U.S. policy and academic circles, there have been proposals for the reduction of the USN aircraft carrier force, in view of the need for platforms optimized against emerging threats, such as piracy.[38] These might have fuelled speculation that the Seventh Fleet force structure would have to be scaled down. This is not the case, however, since over the years before, during, and after the Bush administration, the Seventh Fleet force structure remained more or less unchanged, as Table 8.1 shows. In fact, there are even plans to augment this force, probably in upgrading some of its assets to suit the operating environment of the Asia-Pacific littorals better.[39] Notably, the Seventh Fleet started bolstering its capabilities in 2009, ostensibly to meet a range of threats emanating from North Korea and China's naval buildup.[40] The American resolve to maintain its naval dominance in the region has also been

TABLE 8.1

U.S. Navy Seventh Fleet Force Structure, 2002–10

Year	Number of ships in inventory			
	Aircraft carrier	Principal surface combatants[a]	Large command ship	Principal amphibious assault vessels[b]
2002	1	6–9	1	4
2003	1	6–9	1	4
2004	1	9	1	4
2005	1	9	1	4
2006	1	8	1	4
2007	1	10	1	4
2008	1 (nuclear)	10	1	4
2009	1 (nuclear)	10	1	4
2010	1 (nuclear)	10	1	2

Notes:
a. Principal surface combatants refers to warships of frigate size and above.
b. Principal amphibious assault vessels refer to those classified as landing ship, tank (LST) and above.
Source: Successive annual publications of the International Institute for Strategic Studies, The Military Balance (London, New York: Routledge, 2002–10).

manifested in its deployment of three cruise-missile submarines to the Seventh Fleet to bolster its firepower significantly.[41] It seems highly likely that the U.S. military — notwithstanding the swirling concerns of its commitment to the Asia-Pacific — is here to stay for quite some time due to the United States' long-standing regional security stakes.[42]

The ASEAN response to the Obama administration's policy approach has been rather more relaxed, in contrast to the relative sense of unease during the Bush administration. In fact, the toning down of the GWOT rhetoric by the Obama administration seems to have removed, to a significant extent, the socio-political contradictions faced by ASEAN governments with respect to their domestic constituencies (particularly in Muslim ASEAN states). It has thus paved a smoother path for improved U.S. military relations with the region. Indeed, the growing ease and comfort of ASEAN states about the U.S. military role can be observed in the recent decision by Malaysia to participate in the Cobra Gold military exercise in 2010, after being an observer in previous years.[43] Also, Malaysia and Thailand joined for the first time the United States–led "Rim of the Pacific" (RIMPAC) exercise in June 2010.[44] While U.S. military roles in Southeast Asia will be more or less similar to those that existed under the Bush administration, the relaxation of the U.S.-ASEAN cooperative climate has also eased further enhancements, such as the revival of lost key partnerships, with particular respect to Indonesia for instance.[45] A notable development has been the recent lifting of an arms embargo by Washington on the Indonesian military.[46] But prior to this, however, the higher echelons of the Indonesian political and military establishment had expressed ambivalence towards the prospects of enhanced U.S.-Indonesian military relations. Top Indonesian defence and military officials had reportedly declared that Jakarta would not be pleading with the United States for defence and military cooperation, notwithstanding the intensification of such cooperation since 2008.[47] With the emphasis on promoting multilateral cooperation, given the U.S. financial and military force constraints, interoperability of forces between the United States and ASEAN countries and capacity building will be promoted more strongly — this time being relatively more targeted at urgent needs, particularly NTS risks, for which ASEAN military forces on the whole remain inadequately prepared. Washington appears willing to assist in bolstering ASEAN capacity in dealing with non-military contingencies, such as natural disasters. This is keenly welcomed. For instance, in April 2010, Kuala Lumpur publicly proposed the idea of furthering collaboration with the United States in disaster management.[48] At least, when ASEAN military capacities are in the process of being strengthened against NTS risks, the Seventh Fleet — which had aptly demonstrated its unsurpassed ability to respond rapidly to humanitarian crises, such as the tsunami in December 2004[49] — will continue to be seen as a valuable force. It will continue to serve as a deterrent against hostile emerging regional powers, or to project "soft military power"[50] where ASEAN capacity falls short.

U.S.-ASEAN MILITARY RELATIONS: "BUSINESS AS USUAL" AND FUTURE PROSPECTS

After years of neglect and notwithstanding the conflicting signals shown by Washington,[51] Southeast Asia remains a key component in U.S. policy towards the Asia-Pacific. Contrary to what some observers have suggested, the United States has always had a deep interest in Southeast Asia and in developing a more active military presence in the region.[52] ASEAN continues to view the United States as a key security partner. ASEAN Secretary-General Surin Pitsuwan has stated that "the United States is very important to ASEAN as well as the world.... It has the power, large market, centre of creativity, influence and military might that can be useful for others."[53] Key to continued, viable U.S. military presence in the Asia-Pacific is the basing rights in Japan. The periodic controversies surrounding the relocation of U.S. military forces on the island of Okinawa appear to have created some worries in Southeast Asia. For instance, Singapore's Minister Mentor Lee Kuan Yew urged the maintenance of U.S. military bases in Japan when he opined in May 2010, "We believe that their [U.S. military bases in Japan] presence brings about stability and peace. They need a base in the northeast, and if there is no base in Japan, they can't deploy their weaponry and project their power. If Japan closes them off from Okinawa, I think it will be a setback for the deployment of the American forces, which is not to the benefit of Asia."[54] This view is most likely shared by many other leaders, not just in Southeast Asia. The loss of military basing in Japan will adversely affect the ability of U.S. forces to negotiate the vast geographical distances of the Asia-Pacific, and limit their ability to project viable force for both military and non-military operational purposes. ASEAN leaders are likely aware of this and, for this reason, they hope for the maintenance of the U.S.-Japan security alliance to facilitate continued U.S. military presence in the region.

To be sure, ASEAN sentiments towards the U.S. military presence in the Asia-Pacific may not always reflect those towards direct U.S. military involvement in Southeast Asia itself. U.S.-ASEAN military relations during the Bush administration were focused, almost single-mindedly, on GWOT, and the unilateralist approach adopted by Washington at that time was regarded with considerable animosity by some ASEAN states. The coming of the Obama administration to power signalled a relaxation of ASEAN sentiments towards U.S. military involvement in the region. In particular, Washington's professed intention to emphasize multilateral cooperation, which is in line with a fiscally sustainable doctrine that takes into account the prevailing financial and force constraints, is much welcomed. Nevertheless, the constraints faced by the United States have also brought about concerns that the United States is experiencing a decline and, thus, unable to fulfil its security commitments to the Asia-Pacific as a whole. This may be a rather unwarranted cause for concern, given the continued emphasis Washington places on at least maintaining a viable military detachment in the region as a stabilizing force. However, as far as ASEAN is concerned, no chance has been taken in this regard. While ASEAN generally welcomes the stated desire of Washington to re-engage the region, it appears also acutely aware of the United States' limitations and its own intraregional challenges. In the face of prevailing uncertainties with respect to the multifaceted regional security environment, ASEAN states are either individually or collectively hedging in response.

On a collective basis, ASEAN continues to stress regional community building, the centrepiece being the eventual realization of an ASEAN Community.[55] In fact, there had been urgent calls for the immediate implementation of the APSC (ASEAN Political-Security

Community) Blueprint by some ASEAN members — Vietnam in particular.[56] On the broader front, ASEAN continues to strive to retain its position as driver of the regional security architecture. This is illustrated in the recent creation of a new ASEAN-led defence cooperation mechanism, the ASEAN Plus Eight Defence Ministers Meeting, which is regarded as a move by the regional group to retain its leading role in maintaining regional peace and stability.[57] Within ASEAN itself, there are signs of increased collaboration to enhance collective capacities for dealing with emerging security risks — again with particular respect to NTS issues that have gained salience in the region. In 2007, ASEAN defence ministers issued a joint declaration designed to enhance cooperation in tackling emerging NTS threats, and to provide a framework for dialogue and decision making in the collective ASEAN defence sector.[58] During the 6th ASEAN Air Chiefs Conference in August 2009, Brunei's Deputy Defence Minister, Mohammad Yasmin Umar, stressed the need for collective responses — through enhancing collaboration of ASEAN air forces — to common threats, especially NTS risks.[59] Another instance of initiatives to promote regional collective resilience against security threats has been the agreement reached in principle by ASEAN members to establish a defence industry council akin to the European example, with one of the key aims being the reduction of dependence on the outside world for defence materials.[60] There have been calls for formal military cooperation. Malaysia's Defence Minister Datuk Seri Ahmad Zahid Hamidi advocated more joint ASEAN military exercises to bolster defence and security in the region.[61] Whether this will be realized remains to be seen, given the financial and technical disparities among ASEAN countries and the residual intramural rivalries. At least there is some consensus within ASEAN on the need to pool resources to combat NTS threats. ASEAN countries have agreed to deploy military assets to conduct humanitarian and disaster relief (HADR) under the auspices of a new intraregional special task force created for that purpose.[62] From these developments it can be concluded that ASEAN continues to adopt a "business as usual" approach by strategically hedging, perhaps in cognizance of the possible reduction of U.S. security commitments to the region, as a result of budgetary and security preoccupations elsewhere.

However, this concern might have been exaggerated. As seen in successive policy documents and actions taken by Washington, American security interests in the Asia-Pacific — and Southeast Asia — will most likely remain crucial to U.S. policymakers. The United States is not about to withdraw massively from the region. On the contrary, it has shown resolve in addressing prevailing security threats. The U.S. stance towards North Korea's nuclear weapons programme and the sinking of the South Korean corvette *ROKS Cheonan* represents one example of continued U.S. security interest in the region. The U.S. commitment to being a guardian of the South China Sea maritime interests can be seen in its continued quest to sustain military operations, even to the point of risking confrontation with China. This has been a consistent policy that existed before the Bush administration. One needs no reminder about the Sino-U.S. naval stand-offs in 2001 (involving a USN EP-3 Aries-II reconnaissance aircraft operating off Hainan island, where Chinese military activities were thought to be intensifying), and 2009 (two surface stand-offs between U.S. surveillance vessels and alleged Chinese patrol boats, again off Hainan island). On the traditional security front, ASEAN can be reassured, even in view of the increased assertiveness shown by Beijing with regard to the long-standing South China Sea territorial disputes. ASEAN collectively cannot muster sufficient defence capacity against a determined external aggressor. Hence, it requires a viable and willing balancing force that the U.S. military is able to offer. On the NTS front, ASEAN states are aware of their capacity limitations and, while intensifying efforts to bolster intraregional self-reliance in this regard, have tended to regard U.S. willingness to assist in this area positively. ASEAN fears of overreliance on U.S. military help, however, will continue to limit cooperation to slightly more than existing structures. Nonetheless, NTS issues may possibly allow U.S.-ASEAN military cooperation to see new light, particularly with the relaxation of ASEAN's general sentiments towards Washington as a result of the moderate, inclusive approach adopted by the Obama administration.

Because of past and present developments in U.S.-ASEAN military relations, the following policy recommendations may be suggested for ASEAN. First of all, it must be noted that notwithstanding continued U.S. commitment towards Asia-Pacific security and stability, ASEAN countries will assume strategic hedging through multiple channels, the way a group of small and middle powers, relatively resource-constrained and exposed to a multitude of vulnerabilities, will typically do. What Washington may do, other than assuming its security commitments to the region as a stabilizing force, is to help moderate the extent of hedging, especially in the area of military capacity building where inherent risks exist. The gradual financial recovery post-1997/98 marked the revival of military modernization in Southeast Asia. This continued unabated right into the beginning of the new century. Despite the stated focus on counterterrorism, major ASEAN militaries have acquired power projecting capabilities (see Table 8.2). These have been attributed to the need to prepare against emergent NTS issues, such as the protection of SLOCs against pirates, and also for HADR. However, the same types of platforms — such as major surface combatants and large amphibious assault vessels — can be used for both NTS missions and for aggression against neighbouring states. This can be a cause for concern in light of the long-standing territorial and maritime boundary disputes that exist among ASEAN states and with external parties, particularly China.

Washington should continue to reassure ASEAN states, through policy statements and actions, of its continued commitment to stabilizing regional maritime security and to fulfil niche roles in large-scale HADR contingencies. It can encourage ASEAN countries to maintain non-provocative defence[63] postures that call for the

TABLE 8.2
Key Trends in Arms Procurements in the 2000s, Selected ASEAN Countries[a]

Indonesia	4 SIGMA corvettes;[b] 5 Makassar landing platform docks; 6 Su-30KI multirole jet fighters; 2 Kilo-II, and 2 Amur diesel-electric powered submarines (planned)
Malaysia	2 Improved-Lekiu frigates; 6 Kedah (MEKO) offshore patrol vessels; 2 Scorpene diesel-electric powered submarines; 18 Su-30MKM multirole jet fighters; 2 landing platform docks/multipurpose support vessels (planned)
Singapore	6 Formidable frigates; 4 Endurance landing platform docks; 2 Vastergotland diesel-electric powered submarines; 20+ F-16D Block-52D and 24 F-15SG multirole jet fighters
Thailand	2 Pattani frigates; 1-2 landing platform docks (planned); 6 Gripen multirole jet fighters
Vietnam	2 Gepard frigates; 10 Tarantul-III corvettes; 6 Kilo-II diesel-electric powered submarines; 12 Su-30MK2 multirole jet fighters

Notes

a. SIPRI Arms Transfers' Database Online; <http://www.sipri.org/databases/armstransfers> (accessed 30 June 2010). The aftermath of the December 2004 tsunami exposed the inadequacies of rapid response capacities, especially large amphibious vessels capable of rapid response to disaster-hit zones, and may have spurred a region-wide interest in acquiring such ships, especially landing platform docks. The utility of such assets has been aptly demonstrated by not just the U.S. Navy during the disaster relief process, but also the Republic of Singapore Navy and its fleet of landing platform docks which were first to arrive in Sumatran waters in the immediate aftermath of the tsunami.

b. Twenty more low-cost missile corvettes of the same class, under Indonesia's Nasional Korvet Plan (NKP), are envisaged, though subject to funding. See *Naval Forces*, XXX:3 (2009), p. 145. However, funding for such a huge programme may be found wanting. Nonetheless, the Indonesian Navy has recently placed an order for three more *SIGMA* class corvettes from the Netherlands. See, "Indonesia to Purchase Three More Corvettes from Netherlands", *BBC Monitoring Asia Pacific*, 22 June 2010.

minimization of military capabilities[64] that can be perceived to be destabilizing, despite their possible utility in NTS operations. With that, ASEAN states can gear their defence capacity towards a strategy predominantly based on denial, without necessarily posing threats to others. The U.S. military may help bolster the surveillance capacities of ASEAN military forces to the point where the latter is able to take over most, if not all, the surveillance tasks in which the USN is traditionally engaged in the South China Sea.[65] The pooling of individual countries' minimal force projection capacities for NTS contingency response should also be encouraged, in conjunction with external parties, such as the United States, by leveraging the latter's comparative advantage in such capabilities. In accomplishing this, ASEAN states may be able to maintain a credible deterrent, preserve a minimal but viable force-projecting capacity for NTS contingencies, and yet mitigate the likelihood of a classic security dilemma intraregionally and with respect to external parties. This force-oriented approach, of course, has to be complemented by continued efforts in regional confidence building through dialogue and the setting up of formal institutions. With respect to the emergence of China and India as regional military powers, ASEAN and the United States should encourage these two giants to participate more actively in burden sharing. A suggestion worth considering is for ASEAN to engage China and India in managing NTS risks, using their nascent but rapidly-expanding military capacities. This not only helps in bolstering regional capacity collectively against NTS contingencies, but can also have the by-product of mitigating misperceptions of their military power through the "soft" application of "hard" power. Such an integrative approach may, on the one hand, underpin sustainable U.S.-ASEAN military relations and, on the other hand, mitigate the underlying risks stemming from hedging by ASEAN.

Notes

1. The author sincerely thanks the Institute of Southeast Asian Studies for granting him the opportunity to present this chapter. He would also like to extend his gratitude to Dr Bernard Loo, Associate Professor at the S. Rajaratnam School of International Studies (RSIS), Nanyang Technological University, for his comments on this chapter.
2. According to a climate change vulnerability mapping study, climate hazard hotspots

identified in Southeast Asia include the Mekong region of Vietnam, Bangkok and its surrounding environs, the Philippines as well as the western and eastern parts of Java in Indonesia. See Arief Anshory Yusuf and Herminia A. Francisco, "Climate Change Vulnerability Mapping for Southeast Asia", *Economy and Environment Programme for Southeast Asia* (January 2009).

3. Robert Sutter, "The Obama Administration and U.S. Policy in Asia", *Contemporary Southeast Asia* 31, no. 2 (August 2009): 194.

4. Alice Ba, "Systemic Neglect? A Reconsideration of U.S.-Southeast Asia Policy", *Contemporary Southeast Asia* 31, no. 3 (December 2009): 373–74.

5. "U.S. Eyes Indonesia, Vietnam as Potential Strategic Allies in Southeast Asia", Agence France Presse, 1 May 2005.

6. Ba, "Systemic Neglect?", p. 376. See also, Satu P. Limaye, "United States-ASEAN Relations on ASEAN's Fortieth Anniversary: A Glass Half Full", *Contemporary Southeast Asia* 29, no. 3 (December 2007): 462–63.

7. Ba, "Systemic Neglect?", pp. 377–79. See also Amitav Acharya and See Seng Tan, "Betwixt Balance and Community: America, ASEAN, and the Security of Southeast Asia", *International Relations of the Asia-Pacific* 6 (2006): 49–50.

8. These areas of responsibilities include Europe, Northeast Asia, the East Asian littoral (which is defined as the region stretching from south of Japan through Australia and into the Bay of Bengal), the Middle East and South-west Asia. The essence of U.S. military strategy in contributing to economic well-being remains, such as securing access to key markets and strategic resources, and maintaining the security of international sea, air, and space and lines of communication. See, *2001 Quadrennial Defense Review Report*, United States Department of Defense, 30 September 2001, p. 2 <http://www.defense. gov/pubs/pdfs/qdr2001.pdf> (accessed 29 June 2010).

9. See, *2006 Quadrennial Defense Review Report*, United States Department of Defense, 6 February 2006, pp. 29–30 <http://www.defense.gov/qdr/report/Report20060203. pdf> (accessed 29 June 2010).

10. The four areas are Europe, the Middle East, the East Asian Littoral, and Northeast Asia, as regularly emphasized in previous *QDRs*. Ibid, p. 36.

11. See, *2001 QDR*, p. 4.

12. ASEAN remains highly sensitive towards U.S. military presence in the region. Since the withdrawal of U.S. troops from the Philippines in the early 1990s, the U.S. military has been seeking ways to maintain its forward presence in the region. One of the ideas has been the proposal of floating arsenals around its bases near Southeast Asia for use in the region — an idea which was initiated after Bangkok rejected, out of concern of neighbouring countries' sentiments, a proposal by Washington to place equipment onboard commercial ships anchored off Thailand. See "Thailand Says U.S. Can't Place Ships off Coast", *The Record*, 4 November 1994, and "U.S. Mulls 'Floating Arsenal' for Southeast Asia", Reuters News, 20 March 1995.

13. Slobodan Lekic, "Anti-terror Pact with Southeast Asia will not Involve U.S. Ground Troops, Powell Says", Associated Press Newswires, 1 August 2002. Also, in 2003, Admiral Thomas B. Fargo, then commander of PACOM, stressed that the United States would

not reopen military bases in Southeast Asia or redeploy its troops in the region, but would instead bolster joint training exercises to support the war on terror. See "U.S. will not Reopen Military Bases, Realign Troops in Southeast Asia — Fargo", Agence France Presse, 3 June 2003.

14. Lekic, "Anti-terror Pact with Southeast Asia".

15. For instance, then Malaysian Defence Minister Najib Tun Razak warned that the use of U.S. forces in Southeast Asia to fight terrorism would fuel Islamic fanaticism in the region and potentially generate huge socio-political instability. See "U.S. Forces in Southeast Asia will Fuel Islamic Fanaticism: Malaysia Minister", Agence France Presse, 5 June 2004.

16. *The National Security Strategy of the United States of America*, The White House, Washington D.C., United States of America, September 2002, pp. 6 and 15 <http://georgewbush-whitehouse.archives.gov/nsc/nss/2002/nss.pdf> (accessed 20 June 2010).

17. Even before the Bush administration, then U.S. Defence Secretary William Cohen cautioned in 1998 that Southeast Asian nations should not expect the United States to accept limitations on the movements of its naval and other forces in the area, claiming that such demands would amount to unacceptable shackles on U.S. military planning that could present a major problem in times of sudden military trouble, adding that the value of its military presence to regional stability depends upon its operational flexibility. See, Robert Burns, "Cohen Says U.S. Won't Accept Limit on Military Movements in Asia", Associated Press, 12 January 1998.

18. The Philippines, one of the major non-NATO allies to the United States, expressed similar concerns when the Arroyo administration deemed any U.S. missile attack in her country without consent from Manila an intrusion into the country's national sovereignty. In "Malaysia Rules out Yemen-style U.S. Military Action", Agence France-Presse, 11 November 2002.

19. "Southeast Asia Prefers Low Profile Military Cooperation with U.S." Agence France Presse, 13 June 2006.

20. "Crack U.S. Troops May Be Used to Flush Out Terrorists in Key Southeast Asian Waterway", Agence France Presse, 4 April 2004.

21. Of the ASEAN littoral states, Indonesia and Malaysia are the most vocal in opposing the idea of involving the United States in the security of the Malacca Strait. Singapore, however, was interested in this possibility as it deemed it a responsibility for all users — intraregional and extraregional alike — to share in safeguarding security in the strategic waterway. See "RI Official Says Security in Malacca Strait is Littoral Countries' Responsibility", LKBN ANTARA, 9 October 2008; "Malaysia Says U.S. Intervention in Malacca Straits could Create Problems", Agence France Presse, 10 May 2004, and; "Indonesia Reiterates Opposition to Foreign Powers Patrolling Malacca Strait", Agence France Presse, 2 March 2005.

22. Limaye, "United States-ASEAN Relations on ASEAN's Fortieth Anniversary: A Glass Half Full", p. 460.

23. Quoted in Abdul Khalik, "U.S. Maintains Presence in Asia-Pacific", *Jakarta Post*, 26 August 2008.

24. The U.S. Department of Defense also made the decision to increase the presence of the U.S. Navy aircraft carrier battle groups in the Western Pacific and explore the options for homeporting an additional three to four surface combatants and SSGNs in the area, besides maintaining its critical bases in Northeast Asia to serve the additional role of hubs for power projection in future contingencies in other areas of the world. See *2001 QDR*, September 2001, p. 27.

25. David A. Fulghum, Amy Butler, "Air Force Tanker Choice Underscores U.S. Shift to Pacific", *Aerospace Daily & Defense Report* 225, no. 46 (7 March 2008). The uncertain security situation on the Korean Peninsula, however, had recently prompted a rethink of relocating the marine force to Guam. See Satoshi Ogawa, "U.S. Rethinks Marine Corps' Shift to Guam/Wants to Keep Command Unit in Okinawa", *Daily Yomiuri*, 3 July 2010.

26. Most states on mainland Southeast Asia — primarily Cambodia, Laos, and Vietnam — may have reservations about increased U.S. involvement. On the other hand, Indonesia, Singapore and Thailand are pleased.

27. This happened not long after the Sino-U.S. naval incident in the South China Sea, near the PLAN base located on Hainan Island, in March and May the same year. See Danny Kemp, "Return of Prodigal U.S. Pleases Asia", Agence France Presse, 24 July 2009.

28. Sutter, "The Obama Administration", p. 212.

29. As the world is gradually recovering from the global financial recession, the Obama administration expressed its concern over boosting economic growth and restoring order in the American fiscal house, considered as its core national security priorities. This preoccupation also coincides with an increased emphasis on expanding partnerships beyond the traditional U.S. allies and the sharing of the international burden with rising powers such as China and India. See 2010 *National Security Strategy*, White House, Washington D.C., United States of America, May 2010 <http://www.whitehouse. gov/sites/default/files/rss_viewer/national_security_strategy.pdf> (accessed 18 June 2010). Also see "UPDATE 2 — Obama Security Doctrine Stresses Diplomacy, Economy", Reuters News, 27 May 2010.

30. "Commander Keating says, Asia-Pacific Importance Increasing", U.S. Fed News, 16 September 2009.

31. See 2010 *Quadrennial Defense Review Report*, United States Department of Defense, February 2010, pp 65–66 <http://www.defense.gov/qdr/images/QDR_as_of_12Feb10_1000.pdf> (accessed 20 June 2010).

32. Ibid., p. 59.

33. "New U.S. Defense Strategy to Focus on Energy, Climate Change", Kyodo News, 7 June 2010. Current U.S. Chief of Naval Operations Admiral Gary Roughead also stressed that the USN could not work unilaterally or even bilaterally to protect the seas from non-traditional security risks, such as piracy and illicit activities, thus the continued need for broader maritime partnerships — formal and informal — worldwide. This seems to imply a U.S. desire to cooperate more closely with ASEAN states in the maritime NTS realm. See Zachary M. Peterson, "CNO: Broad Maritime Partnerships Essential to Future Maritime Security", *Inside the Navy* 23, no. 25 (28 June 2010).

34. "Disaster Management to Redefine U.S. role in RP, ASEAN", Philippines News Agency, 11 November 2009.
35 Andrew Shearer, "Will America Defend Its Asian Allies? The Pentagon's Quadrennial Defense Review Raises Some Serious Questions", *Wall Street Journal*, 4 February 2010.
36. Ibid.
37. "Obama's Asia Policy: Old Wine in a New Bottle?" *Jakarta Post*, 10 February 2009.
38. See, for instance, Sandra I. Erwin, "A Navy with Fewer Aircraft Carrier No Longer Unthinkable", *National Defense* 91, no. 640 (1 March 2007), and Michael Austin, "Asia's Troubled Waters; The U.S. Navy will have to Face New Challenges from China and North Korea with Fewer Resources", *Wall Street Journal*, 20 May 2010.
39. It is probable that the overall force structure of the U.S. Navy Seventh Fleet will remain roughly similar. The assets will remain geared towards long-range power projection, such as the use of major surface combatants, including the aircraft carrier, all of which will not only serve the traditional warfare roles, but will also be used for NTS missions, such as counter-piracy and HADR. In view of their usefulness in HADR missions, amphibious warfare assets may become another focus area of force augmentation. Nonetheless, there may be a focus towards more specialized platforms optimized to the operational context characterizing Asia-Pacific littorals. For instance, the RIMPAC 2010 exercises have been tipped to test the performance of the Littoral Combat Ship (LCS), *USS Freedom*. Its successful deployment may signal a gradual build-up of such forces in the region to allow the USN to fulfil littoral missions more effectively. See "RIMPAC 2010 Aims to Test Freedom's Capabilities in Shallow Seas", *Inside the Navy* 23, no. 27 (12 July 2010).
40. These improvements include extensive aircraft upgrades, submarine deployments, and an effort to double the fleet's mine countermeasures capabilities through the addition of more ships and helicopters. See Greg Torode, "As Regional Tensions Rise, the U.S. Ensures it will Outmuscle Rivals for Years to Come: America Sends a Signal to Both Allies and Neighbours by Increasing Naval Presence", *South China Morning Post*, 27 May 2010.
41. The three cruise missile submarines are converted Ohio class ballistic missile submarines, and altogether carry a total of 462 Tomahawk land-attack cruisemissiles. See Greg Torode, "U.S. Submarines Emerge in Show of Military Might", *South China Morning Post*, 4 July 2010.
42. "Military Presence in Asia Deemed Critical to Future of U.S. Security", *Inside the Navy* 18, no. 39 (October 2005).
43. "Malaysia to Join Cobra Gold Military Exercises", Agence France Presse, 3 June 2010.
44. "Malaysia, Thailand Join U.S.-led Exercises", Agence France Presse, 25 June 2010.
45. In fact, the Obama administration, since arriving in power, has eyed Indonesia as a key ally due to the country's size of population and moderate brand of Islam. See Shaun Tandon, "Obama Eyes Indonesia as Key U.S. Ally", Agence France Presse, 19 February 2009.
46. "U.S. Has Ended Lethal Weapon Sales Ban: RI", *Jakarta Post*, 5 July 2010.
47. This statement represents one of the strongest sentiments ever made within the

Indonesian military-political circles. See, "RI Will Not Beg to U.S." LKBN ANTARA, 14 June 2010.

48. Besides disaster management, Kuala Lumpur also wanted the U.S. Navy to share expertise in tackling piracy. See "Malaysia Hopes to Collaborate with U.S. in Handling Natural Disasters", BBC Monitoring Asia Pacific, 17 April 2010.

49. See Sutter, "The Obama Administration", p. 206. Derek Mitchell, a member of the Centre for Strategic and International Studies, a Washington-based think tank, remarked that the U.S. military bases, particularly in Okinawa, provided resources which were rapidly tapped for the humanitarian effort post-tsunami, adding that the United States has this unique capability to move rapidly with its military to take care of humanitarian and other security challenges in Asia. In the absence of this capability which is not nearly there in Asia, the United States plays this indispensable role. See "U.S. Eyes Greater Military Clout in Asia following Tsunami Tragedy", Agence France Presse, 5 January 2005.

50. "Soft military power" refers to engaging in non-traditional security tasks, such as humanitarian and disaster relief operations. See, for instance, Patrick M. Mayerchak, "Enhancing Regional Security in Southeast Asia: The Role of America's "Soft Military Power", paper presented for the 48th Annual International Studies Association (ISA) Annual Convention, Chicago, Illinois, United States of America, 28 February–3 March 2007.

51. For example, in 2005, then U.S. Secretary of State Condoleezza Rice's absence from the ASEAN Regional Forum meeting was regarded as a snub to ASEAN, but Washington later sought to clarify this by emphasizing the continued importance of Southeast Asia to the United States. The same point was stressed in 2007 when Deputy State Secretary John Negroponte stated that the United States considers its relations with ASEAN a critical component in its dealings with East Asia as a whole. See "Southeast Asia Remains Important to the U.S.: Zoellick", Agence France Presse, 28 July 2005, and "U.S. Says 'Committed' to SE Asia", Agence France Presse, 1 August 2007.

52. For instance, in 2001, then commander of the U.S. Air Force mobility command, General Charles Robertson, remarked that the United States would require access to larger bases in Southeast Asia to project military power across the Asia-Pacific, should U.S. strategy shift to the region, citing the need to overcome "the tyranny of distance" in the Asia-Pacific. See "U.S. General Foresees Need for Access to Larger Bases in SE Asia if Strategy Shifts", Agence France Presse, 19 June 2001.

53. "Roundup: U.S. Regards ASEAN as Key to Solution of Future Problems", Xinhua News Agency, 11 June 2010.

54. Quoted in "U.S. Military Presence Crucial to Balance of Power in Asia", Channel News Asia, 20 May 2010.

55. The ASEAN Community comprises three pillars, namely, political-security, economic, and socio-cultural. In fact, the idea of a "security community" was suggested by the United States back in 2000. During that time, Commander of the U.S. Pacific Command Admiral Dennis Blair proposed the establishment of a security community in Southeast Asia to solve common military challenges and promote peace in the region. See "U.S.

Proposes to Set Up Southeast Asia Security Community", Xinhua News Agency, 2 October 2000. In 2009, as stated in the ASEAN Political-Security Community (APSC) Blueprint, ASEAN leaders expressed their desire for the grouping to become a European Union–like community eventually by 2015. This Blueprint calls for an early warning system based on existing mechanisms to prevent the occurrence/escalation of conflicts while intensifying cooperation among the military forces within ASEAN. See "ASEAN Goal: To be Like EU", *Philippine Daily Inquirer*, 1 March 2009. See also *ASEAN Political-Security Blueprint*, Association of Southeast Asian Nations (Jakarta: ASEAN Secretariat, 2009) <http://www.aseansec.org/5187-18.pdf> (accessed 22 June 2010).

56. "Vietnam Calls for 'Immediate' Implementation of ASEAN Security Blueprint", BBC Monitoring Asia Pacific, 11 April 2009.

57. Lee Seok Kwai and Jermyn Chow, "Strong Backing for ASEAN Plus Eight Security Forum", *Straits Times*, 7 June 2010. The eight non-ASEAN partners are Australia, China, India, Japan, New Zealand, South Korea, Russia, and the United States.

58. "ASEAN Defence Ministers Sign Joint Declaration to Deepen Cooperation", Channel News Asia, 14 November 2007.

59. "ASEAN Air Forces Called for Collaboration", Xinhua News Agency, 12 August 2009.

60. "ASEAN Plans Defence Industry Council", Organisation of Asia-Pacific News Agencies, 3 November 2009.

61. See "ASEAN should Cooperate to Beef up Defence", *New Straits Times*, 15 May 2010, and "ASEAN to Discuss Formal Military Cooperation in May — Malaysian Minister", BBC Monitoring Asia Pacific, 18 February 2010. The Malaysian Defence Minister remains optimistic despite being mindful of the technological and financial disparities among ASEAN member states. See, "ASEAN Needs to Find Common Areas to Forge Defence Cooperation", Organisation of Asia-Pacific News Agencies, 22 April 2010.

62. "ASEAN Agrees on Use of Military Assets for Disaster Relief", BBC Monitoring Asia Pacific, 26 February 2009. Vietnamese Prime Minister Nguyen Tan Dung also called on ASEAN to bolster military cooperation — collectively as a grouping, and with external partners — to cope with NTS challenges. See "Vietnam's PM Calls on ASEAN to Expand Military Cooperation", Vietnam News Summary, 26 March 2010. This call was also echoed by the special assistant to the ASEAN Secretary-General, Termsak Chalermpalanupap, who remarked that "ASEAN needs to have defence security cooperation, because of non-traditional security challenges in many areas. In view of those challenges, we need defence and military personnel and equipment." See, "Better Defence Cooperation to Help Build ASEAN Community", Thai News Service, 30 April 2010.

63. The concept of non-provocative defence (NPD) emerged as the Cold War was coming to an end, and was largely advocated by European states. Notable works done in this area include *The Foundations of Defensive Defence*, edited by Anders Boserup and Robert Neild (Basingstoke: MacMillan, 1990); *Nonoffensive Defense: A Global Perspective*, United Nations Institute of Disarmament Research (New York: Taylor & Francis, 1990), in which a chapter on the applicability of the concept on Southeast Asia was discussed; Bjorn Moller and Hakan Wiberg, *Non-Offensive Defence for the Twenty-First Century* (Boulder CO: Westview Press, 1994); and more recently Geoffrey Wiseman, *Concepts of*

Non-provocative Defence: Ideas and Practices in International Security (New York: Palgrave in association with St. Antony's College, Oxford, 2002). It is the author's opinion that such a concept possibly alluded to ASEAN defence discourse and may form a crucial part of the ASEAN discourse on comprehensive security — an overarching concept that forms the basis of ASEAN Community building. A notable document in this respect is the Track-II Council for Security Cooperation in the Asia Pacific (CSCAP) memorandum on comprehensive and cooperative security that revealed elements directly related to the NPD concept. However, whether or not this concept is practised by ASEAN states constitutes part of the author's research inquiry, which is an ongoing work in progress for his doctoral dissertation dealing with Southeast Asian naval developments. See *CSCAP Memorandum No. 3 — The Concepts of Comprehensive Security and Cooperative Security*, Working Group on Comprehensive and Cooperative Security <http://www. cscap.org/uploads/docs/Memorandums/CSCAP%20Memorandum%20No%203%20- -%20The%20Concepts%20of%20Comp%20Sec%20and%20Coop%20Sec.pdf> (accessed 18 August 2009).

64. According to a research survey conducted by the author with a multinational group of naval officers at the Singapore Armed Forces Training Institute (SAFTI), results tabulated showed that certain assets can be regarded as destabilizing. These are force projection assets such as aircraft carriers, major surface combatants (especially those armed with destabilizing weapons such as supersonic cruisemissiles), and large amphibious landing ships. Coastguard-type ships and naval minor surface combatants for instance, by contrast, are regarded as non-destabilizing. Data collected from Research Questionnaire Survey conducted by author at SAFTI, Singapore, 11 June 2010.

65. This may mitigate the risks of further Sino-U.S. naval confrontations, given the contention Beijing has of Washington not being a signatory of the United Nations Convention on the Law of the Sea (1982).

9

UNITED STATES–CHINA RELATIONS

Bo Zhiyue

The relationship between the United States and China is the most important bilateral relationship in the twenty-first century. The status of the bilateral relationship is significant not only for the two most powerful nations, but also for the rest of the world. This relationship has three important characteristics. In political terms, the United States and China are strategic partners. They are two of the most important players in both bilateral and multilateral issues in the world. In economic terms, they are both partners and competitors. In terms of military relations, the two countries are both competitors and partners.

There are some important issues facing the United States and China. Bilaterally, the United States and China will have to address their different concerns. For China, certain issues are concerned with its core interests. These include Taiwan, Tibet, Xinjiang, and the South China Sea. For the United States, China's currency exchange issue and human rights are major concerns. Multilaterally, the United States needs China more than China needs the United States. The

United States needs China's cooperation on nuclear issues in North Korea and Iran, as well as a host of other issues, such as energy security and climate change.

The United States and China have developed some mechanisms to deal with issues of their mutual concerns. These include summit meetings and regular exchanges between top leaders from the two countries, and annual strategic and economic dialogue sessions. These mechanisms have facilitated political communications between the two countries, but have yet to produce more tangible results.

MAIN CHARACTERISTICS OF U.S.-CHINA RELATIONS

Strategic Partnership

Although it is not explicitly spelled out in the joint statement issued by the United States and China in November 2009,[1] the two major powers regard each other as strategic partners. U.S. President Barack Obama has taken China much more seriously than his predecessors. He has indicated on a number of occasions that China is becoming an important global power and that the United States treats China not just as a partner, but as a strategic partner, as reflected in his interview with Reuters on the eve of his first Asia trip on 9 November 2009. In his answer to a question about whether China is a rival or an ally, Obama came to the conclusion that China is a strategic partner. In his words, "it's very hard to see how we succeed or China succeeds in our respective goals without working together. And that is, I think, the purpose of the strategic partnership and that's why this trip to China is going to be so important."[2]

Since he took office as the U.S. President in January 2009, Obama has made extraordinary efforts to work with China. In the past two decades, there has been a tradition in the White House for the incumbent president to meet with the Dalai Lama whenever the latter is present in Washington. From April 1991 to October 2007, three American presidents (George H. Bush, Bill Clinton, and George W. Bush) met with the Dalai Lama altogether eleven times. However, Obama broke the tradition by avoiding the Dalai Lama in October 2009 when the Tibetan monk showed up in the U.S. capital.

On the other hand, China has always taken the United States very seriously and has been trying to develop a strategic partnership with the sole superpower. President Hu Jintao met President George W. Bush sixteen times between 2003 and 2008. China conducted with the United States six rounds of "strategic dialogue" (in Chinese, but "senior dialogue" in English) from August 2005 to December 2008, and five rounds of "strategic economic dialogue" from December 2006 to December 2008.[3]

The "U.S.–China Joint Statement" issued on 17 November 2009 after the Obama-Hu summit devoted a whole section (Part II) on "Building and Deepening Bilateral Strategic Trust". "The United States and China", the statement reads, "have an increasingly broad base of cooperation and share increasingly important common responsibilities on many major issues concerning global stability and prosperity." Therefore, "the two countries", the statement declares, "should further strengthen coordination and cooperation, work together to tackle challenges, and promote world peace, security and prosperity."[4]

Economic Cooperation and Competition between the United States and China

In the past three decades, the United States and China have become economic partners in many areas. Bilateral trade expanded from merely US$2.5 billion in 1979[5] to US$333.7 billion in 2008.[6] In 2008, the United States was China's top trade partner and China was the United States' number two trade partner.[7] China has become one of the most important sources of goods and products in the world for the United States (Figure 9.1). In 1987, Japan exported the most

FIGURE 9.1
Top Trade Partners of the United States

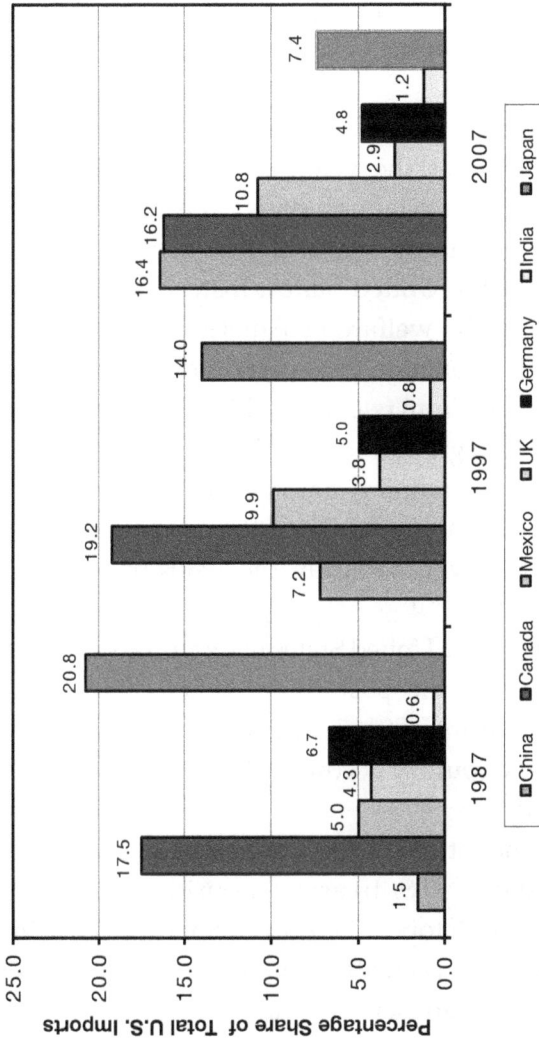

Source: U.S. Census Bureau <http://www.census.gov/foreign-trade/balance/c5700.html#2003> (accessed 15 July 2010).

to the United States. In 1997, Canada became the largest supplier for the United States. And in 2007, China surpassed Canada as the top provider of goods and products for U.S. consumers.[8]

More importantly, China has been rapidly becoming an important market for American products over the past twenty years (Figure 9.2), importing US$3.5 billion in 1987 and US$69.7 billion in 2008.[9]

Although the U.S. trade deficit with China has been an issue of contention over the years,[10] it was no longer a major issue in the U.S.-China relations under the Bush administration. The Americans gradually realized that China is not an economic competitor of the United States. Instead, China has been a major contributor to the welfare of Americans. "China is large enough and competitive enough to cause economic problems for the United States", advisors from two major think tanks in Washington DC (the Center for Strategic and International Studies, and the Institute for International Economics) pointed out in 2006, "but it has neither derailed our economy nor been the chief cause of our difficulties, any more than were Japan in the 1980s or other Asian countries in the early 1990s."[11]

Financially, the United States has become increasingly dependent on China. Over the past thirty years, China's foreign reserve skyrocketed from US$167 million in 1978 to US$1,946 billion in 2008, with the country becoming the top holder of foreign reserves in the world.[12]

In the meantime, China surpassed Japan and became the largest holder of U.S. treasury securities in 2008. Within twelve months, from October 2007 to October 2008, China's holdings of U.S. treasury securities expanded from US$459.1 billion to US$652.9 billion, an increase of almost US$200 billion. In particular, after Lehman Brothers went bankrupt in September 2008, China acquired an additional US$66 billion worth of U.S. treasury securities in October 2008 as a show of its support for the U.S. Government. As of April 2010, China holds US$900.2 billion of

FIGURE 9.2
China's Imports from the United States

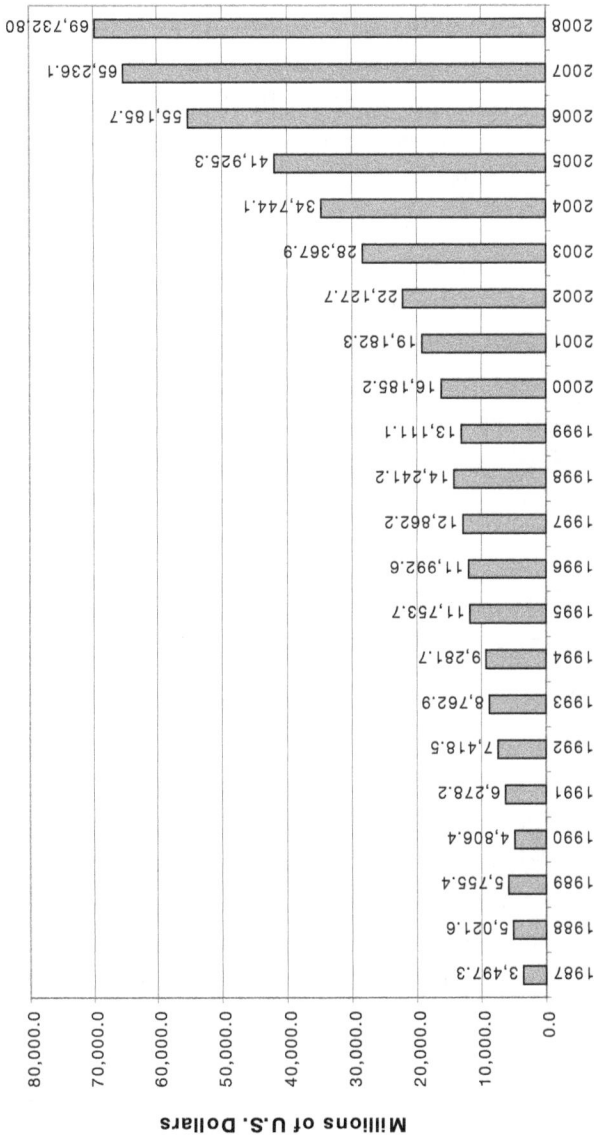

Millions of U.S. Dollars

Year	Value
1987	3,497.3
1988	5,021.6
1989	5,755.4
1990	4,806.4
1991	6,278.2
1992	7,418.5
1993	8,762.9
1994	9,281.7
1995	11,753.7
1996	11,992.6
1997	12,862.2
1998	14,241.2
1999	13,111.1
2000	16,185.2
2001	19,182.3
2002	22,127.7
2003	28,367.9
2004	34,744.1
2005	41,925.3
2006	55,185.7
2007	65,236.1
2008	69,732.80

Source: U.S. Census Bureau <http://www.census.gov/foreign-trade/balance/index.html#C>.

U.S. treasury securities, almost a quarter of the total U.S. treasury securities held by foreigners.[13]

In the aftermath of the U.S. financial crisis, protectionism has become more prevalent in the United States. Since January 2009, the U.S. Department of Commerce has initiated a series of trade subsidy investigations on imports from China. In the first three quarters of 2009, the United States launched fourteen investigations against Chinese products worth US$5.8 billion (639 per cent over the same period in 2008).[14] In particular, President Obama signed an order in September 2009, imposing a 35 per cent tariff on Chinese-made tyre imports over the next three years, in response to a petition from the steelworkers union. One week before Obama's trip to Asia, the United States slapped preliminary anti-dumping duties ranging up to 99 per cent on Chinese-made oil well pipe in the biggest U.S. trade action against China, risking a trade war with its largest supplier.[15]

Military Competition and Cooperation between the United States and China

Apparently, the United States still lacks confidence in China's claim of a peaceful rise. The U.S. military still regards China as a major potential threat. The U.S. air force and navy have been conducting covert operations along China's coast for many years. An American spy plane (EP3) clashed with a Chinese Air Force plane over China's South China Sea in April 2001. *USNS Impeccable*, an American surveillance vessel, intruded into China's exclusive economic zone (EEZ) and clashed with Chinese ships in March 2009.

China, on the other hand, has been trying to cooperate with the United States in military affairs. To facilitate communication and mutual understanding, CMC Vice Chairman General Xu Caihou paid a visit to the United States in October 2009 and reached a seven-point understanding with U.S. Defense Secretary Robert Gates.[16]

MAJOR ISSUES IN U.S.-CHINA RELATIONS

U.S.-China relations are asymmetric. As the sole superpower, the United States needs China not only as a partner in bilateral relations, but also as a global strategic partner on a host of international issues. China, in contrast, is much more concerned with its own core national interests. Their lists of major issues, therefore, may not necessarily overlap completely.

Concerns of the United States

For the United States, there are both bilateral and multilateral issues that need to be addressed with China. Bilaterally, there are three major issues. The first is China's renminbi exchange rate.[17] As it is well known, the U.S. trade deficit with China became a major issue after China replaced Japan as a major exporter to the United States. Senator Charles Schumer introduced a bill (S. 295) on 3 February 2005, claiming that the Chinese currency was undervalued by between 15 per cent and 40 per cent, or an average of 27.5 per cent. He threatened to impose "a rate of duty of 27.5 per cent ad valorem on any article that is the growth, product, or manufacture of the People's Republic of China, imported directly or indirectly into the United States".[18] Under pressure from the United States, China delinked its currency from the U.S. dollar on 21 July 2005. In the aftermath of the global financial crisis, China again pegged its currency to the U.S. dollar.

The Obama administration was very careful in its first year not to provoke China over the renminbi exchange rate issue. During his nomination hearings as the treasury secretary designate, Tim Geithner alleged that China was manipulating its currency and the Obama administration would "use aggressively all the diplomatic avenues" to change China's currency practice.[19] Yet, in the subsequent two semi-annual reports on international economic and exchange rate policies to Congress (in April and October 2009 respectively), the Treasury Department determined that China was not a currency manipulator after all.

One of the reasons the Obama administration was initially cautious about the currency issue with China is that China had been the largest holder of U.S. treasury bills since September 2008 and China's holdings were increasing. According to the U.S. Department of the Treasury, foreigners purchased a total of US$760.4 billion of additional U.S. treasury securities (treasury bills, bonds, notes, and others) between August 2008 and August 2009. In the meantime, China increased its holdings by US$223.4 billion, representing 29.4 per cent of the total additional foreign holdings of the period. By the end of August 2009, China's holdings of U.S. treasury securities amounted to US$797.1 billion, 23.1 per cent of the total foreign holdings (US$3,448.8 billion).[20]

However, the Obama administration became more vocal on China's renminbi exchange rate issue in early 2010. President Obama, for instance, commented on 11 March 2010 that China's movement towards a more market-based currency system "would make an essential contribution to that global rebalancing effort" and that Chinese exchange rate reform was in line with the G-20 goal of boosting consumption and domestic demand in countries that had external surpluses, such as China, and encouraging saving and export in countries with external deficits, such as the United States.[21] In the end, the United States decided to postpone the semi-annual report on international economic and exchange rate policies from 15 April 2010 to a much later date, and China decided to adopt a more flexible exchange rate in June 2010. As a result, the Department of the Treasury did not cite China as a currency manipulator in its report released on 8 July 2010.[22]

The second issue for the United States is trade. For some quarters in the United States, China is to blame for the loss of U.S. jobs. As China was engaged in unfair trade practices such as dumping, U.S. firms lost out, resulting in job losses. The Alliance for American Manufacturing, for instance, claims that American job losses are due to China's unfair and predatory illegal trade practices. Under the title "China Cheats: America Loses", the organization described the problem this way:

> For years, China has been pursuing unfair and predatory illegal trade practices designed to tilt the playing field in their favor. American workers and families have suffered as they have lost their jobs, and now the illegally dumped and subsidized Chinese products that have put them out of work are also now endangering the health and safety of them and their children.... China's cheating skews the market, and American workers, families, and children are paying the price.[23]

The third issue for the United States is that of human rights. Again, the Obama administration maintained a very low profile on this issue in its first year in office. Secretary of State Hillary Clinton talked more about three major crises (global financial crisis, global climate change crisis, and the nuclear issue of North Korea) than about the issue of human rights during her maiden trip to Beijing in February 2009. President Obama similarly avoided the issue of human rights during his trip to China in November 2009. Even Nancy Pelosi, one of the most ardent human rights advocates against China in the United States, and Speaker of the U.S. House of Representatives, was "all smiles and handshakes" during her "climate change" tour of China in May 2009.[24]

However, the Obama administration became critical of China's Internet policies in early 2010. In the midst of a major controversy between an American company, Google, and the Chinese Government, Secretary Clinton intervened on behalf of the American company. After Google declared that it intended to close down its operations in China because it was attacked in China and was not happy about censorship in China,[25] Clinton made a speech on Internet freedom on 21 January 2010, specifically criticizing China.[26]

China's Concerns

In contrast, China is much more concerned with its own core national interests. These include Taiwan, Tibet, Xinjiang, and the South China Sea. The Taiwan issue was one reason U.S.-China relations turned sour in early 2010. On 6 January 2010, the U.S. Department of Defense announced a contract with Lockheed Martin Corp to sell an unspecified number of Patriot missiles to Taiwan. This was part of a US$6.4-billion arms package approved under then U.S. President George W. Bush in late 2008. But the Obama administration decided to go ahead with the package.[27]

China swiftly denounced the arms sales and threatened to take strong action against the companies involved. At a press conference on 7 January 2010, Foreign Ministry spokeswoman, Jiang Yu, urged the United States to recognize the "serious harm caused by arms sales to Taiwan" to U.S.-China relations.[28] Rear Admiral Yang Yi, a researcher at the Chinese National Defense University, threatened to impose sanctions on companies that sell weapons to Taiwan.[29]

After the United States announced the full package of arms sales to Taiwan on 29 January 2010, China announced four countermeasures. First, China would suspend high-level visits by military leaders from both sides. Second, China would defer a series of military exchange programmes with the United States. Third, China would postpone the U.S.-China vice-ministerial level talks on strategic security, arms control, and non-proliferation. And most significantly, China would impose sanctions on those U.S. companies that were involved in selling weapons to Taiwan.[30] As Vice–Foreign Minister He Yafei indicated, the Taiwan issue concerns China's sovereignty and territorial integrity, involves China's core interests, concerns the national feelings of the Chinese people, and is the most important and most sensitive issue in U.S.-China relations.[31] To add insult to injury, the Obama administration "trampled on" China's other core interests[32] in the following month when President Obama decided to meet with the Dalai Lama in Washington. Against the

Chinese Government's repeated warnings, Obama met with the visiting Tibetan monk in the map room of the White House on 18 February 2010.[33]

Subsequently, it was revealed that China had made it clear to the United States that the South China Sea was one of China's core interests, in addition to the issues of Taiwan, Tibet, and Xinjiang.[34] It is reported that the Chinese side relayed such a stand to two American visitors, Deputy Secretary of State James Steinberg, and the senior director for Asian affairs at the National Security Council under the White House, Jeff Bader, in March 2010.[35] The caption under a photo showing a Chinese ship and the American surveillance ship, USNS Impeccable, explains the picture as the Chinese ship "expelling" (quzhu) the American ship.

Global Issues in U.S.-China Relations

On global issues, the United States needs China more than China needs the United States because the two countries have different roles in the world. As the sole superpower in the world, the United States feels increasingly inadequate to police other countries. The gap between its ambition for global dominance and its limited resources to do so is increasingly expanding. From this perspective, the Obama administration has decided that it is no longer a good idea to solve global problems through unilateralism and by hard power alone. The United States, as Secretary Clinton put it, must use "smart" power to restore American leadership.[36] And the United States, as President Obama has stressed a number of times, must not work alone but should seek strategic partners for global issues.[37] In this regard, China is the best candidate. The United States needs China's cooperation on nuclear issues in North Korea and Iran, as well as a host of other issues such as energy security and climate change.

On the other hand, China is not yet a global power. It is more concerned about its own core interests than global issues. Moreover, because the Chinese Government has adopted the policy of non-interference, the Chinese leadership is less inclined to advocate certain agendas in its external relations.

CONCLUSION

In a word, the United States and China are strategic partners in political terms and partners and competitors at the same time in economic terms, but they can be potential competitors militarily. Because of the asymmetric nature of the bilateral relationship, the United States needs China more than China needs the United States. In terms of the bilateral relations, the United States is more concerned with China's currency exchange rate issue, the U.S trade deficit, and human rights. China, on the other hand, is much more concerned with issues related to its core national interests, such as Taiwan, Tibet, Xinjiang, and the South China Sea. As a result of the American financial crisis, China has become more assertive about its core interests. The bilateral relations went sour in early 2010 when the Obama administration trampled on China's core interests. In terms of global issues, China is less inclined to take a firm stand against any country because of its non-interference policy while the United States feels increasingly inadequate in handling global issues through military power alone and on its own. The United States would like to employ a combination of hard and soft power (that is, smart power) and seek strategic partners such as China.

The United States and China have developed some mechanisms to deal with issues of their mutual concern. These include summit meetings and regular exchanges between top leaders from the two countries and annual strategic and economic dialogue sessions. These mechanisms have facilitated political communications between the two countries, but have yet to produce more tangible results.

Notes

1. <http://www.whitehouse.gov/the-press-office/us-china-joint-statement> (accessed 15 July 2010).
2. <http://www.reuters.com/article/idUSTRE5A902Q20091110> (accessed 15 July 2010).
3. For details see, Bo Zhiyue, "Obama's China Policy", *China-U.S. Relations: Analytical Approaches and Contemporary Issues*, edited by Guo Sujian (forthcoming).
4. <http://www.whitehouse.gov/the-press-office/us-china-joint-statement> (accessed 15 July 2010).
5. Figures for trade between China and the United States are not available for the period 1979–82. But Premier Wen Jiaobao used this figure for 1979 in his speech delivered at a luncheon hosted by the American Bankers Association in New York on 8 December 2003. See Wen Jiabao, "共同开创中美经贸合作的新局面" [Work Together to Open a New Chapter in U.S.-China Trade and Economic Cooperation], 8 December 2003 <http://www.for68.com/new/2006/7/wu107218362027760024180-0.htm> (accessed 15 July 2010).
6. In 2008, China's exports to the United States were US$252.3 billion (an increase of 8.4 per cent over 2007) and China's imports from the United States were US$81.4 billion (an increase of 17.4 per cent over 2007), with a trade surplus of US$170.9 billion. For details, see <http://www.cacs.gov.cn/zhongmeimaoyi/show.aspx?str1=&articleId=50011> (accessed 15 July 2010).
7. The figure from the U.S. Census Bureau is US$407.5 billion, see <http://www.census.gov/foreign-trade/balance/c5700.html#2008> (accessed 15 July 2010).
8. Although Canada surpassed China in 2008 as the top exporter to the United States, China took over Canada again in 2009 as the largest exporter to the United States. In 2009, the total amount of exports from China to the United States was US$296,373.9 million and the total amount of exports from Canada to the United States was US$226,248.4 million. For details, see <http://www.census.gov/foreign-trade/balance/c5700.html#2009> and <http://www.census.gov/foreign-trade/balance/c1220.html#2009> (accessed 15 July 2010).
9. <http://www.census.gov/foreign-trade/balance/c5700.html#2003> (accessed 15 July 2010).
10. For a detailed analysis of this issue, see Wang Yong, *Zhongmei Jingmao Guanxi* [The Political Economy of China-U.S. Trade Relations] (Beijing: Zhongguo Shichang Chubanshe, 2007), pp. 123–36.
11. C. Fred Bergsten, Bates Gill, Nicholas R. Lardy, and Derek J. Mitchell, *China – The Balance Sheet: What the World Needs to Know Now about the Emerging Superpower* (Washington, D.C.: Public Affairs/IIE/CSIS, 2006), p. 10.

12. For details, see <http://www.safe.gov.cn> and <http://finance.people.com.cn/GB/8671303.html> (accessed 15 July 2010).
13. <http://www.ustreas.gov/tic/mfh.txt> (accessed 15 July 2010).
14. <http://finance.ifeng.com/roll/20091110/1447917.shtml> (accessed 15 July 2010).
15. <http://cn.reuters.com/article/companyNewsEng/idCNN0512983120091105> (accessed 15 July 2010).
16. For details, see Zhiyue, "Obama's China Policy".
17. For an insightful paper from Japan's perspective, see Ronald McKinnon, "Why China Should Keep its Exchange Rate Pegged to the Dollar: A Historical Perspective from Japan", unpublished manuscript, October 2006 <http://www.stanford.edu/~mckinnon/papers/International%20Finance%20China%20peg.pdf> (accessed 15 July 2010).
18. <http://thomas.loc.gov/cgi-bin/query/z?c109:S.295> (accessed 15 July 2010).
19. "Finance Committee Questions for the Record", United States Senate Committee on Finance, Hearing on Confirmation of Mr Timothy F. Geithner to be Secretary of the U.S. Department of Treasury, 21 January 2009, pp. 81, 94.
20. U.S. Department of the Treasury <http://treas.gov/tic/mfh.txt> (accessed 15 July 2010).
21. <http://www.chinaeconomicreview.com/dailybriefing/2010_03_12/Obama:_Chinese_exchange-rate_reform_would_bring_global_benefits.html> (accessed 15 July 2010).
22. <http://www.automatedtrader.net/real-time-news/48116/textus-treasury-does-not-designate-china-fx-manipulator> (accessed 15 July 2010).
23. <http://www.americanmanufacturing.org/issues/china-cheats/how-china-cheats/> (accessed 15 July 2010).
24. Joseph J. Schatz, "Duet With the Dragon: What's Next in U.S.-China Relationship?" CQ Today Online News, 20 June 2009 <http://www.cqpolitics.com/wmspage.cfm?docID=news-000003149630&cpage=1> (accessed 15 July 2010).
25. For details, see <http://wiki.mbalib.com/wiki/Google%E9%80%80%E5%87%BA%E4%B8%AD%E5%9B%BD%E5%B8%82%E5%9C%BA#_note-4> (accessed 15 July 2010).
26. <http://www.state.gov/secretary/rm/2010/01/135519.htm> (accessed 15 July 2010).
27. <http://www.reuters.com/article/idUSTRE6060V020100107> (accessed 15 July 2010).
28. <http://www.fmprc.gov.cn/chn/gxh/tyb/fyrbt/t650234.htm> (accessed 15 July 2010).
29. <http://www.zaobao.com/special/china/sino_us/pages8/sino_us100107.shtml> (accessed 15 July 2010). For a list of U.S. companies involved in the arms sales, see <http://news.qq.com/a/20100130/001228.htm> (accessed 15 July 2010).
30. <http://news.xinhuanet.com/world/2010-01/30/content_12904277.htm> (accessed 15 July 2010). For a collection of articles in Chinese in this regard, see <http://military.people.com.cn/GB/8221/51755/181011/.
31. <http://www.mfa.gov.cn/chn/gxh/tyb/zyxw/t654807.htm> (accessed 15 July 2010).
32. These comments were made by U.S. Ambassador John Huntsman in an interview in May 2010 <http://timesofindia.indiatimes.com/home/opinion/edit-page/Shadow-Boxing-In-Beijing/articleshow/5931537.cms> (accessed 15 July 2010).
33. <http://www.reuters.com/article/idUSN1116932520100218> (accessed 15 July 2010).

34. <http://news.xinhuanet.com/mil/2010-07/05/content_13809645.htm> (accessed 15 July 2010).

35. <http://english.peopledaily.com.cn/90001/90780/91342/6906359.html> (accessed 15 July 2010).

36. <http://www.timesonline.co.uk/tol/news/world/us_and_americas/article5510049. ece> (accessed 15 July 2010).

37. <http://www.whitehouse.gov/the-press-office/remarks-president-barack-obama-suntory-hall> (accessed 15 July 2010).

10

SHIFT IN U.S. POLICY TOWARDS MYANMAR

U Myint Soe

In September 2009, the United States announced a new course in its policy towards Myanmar following a seven-month review undertaken by the Obama administration. Recognizing that decades of pursuing policies of isolation and sanctions had done little to influence change among Myanmar's military leaders, the United States decided to maintain its sanctions on Myanmar while simultaneously undertaking direct dialogue with senior leaders of the regime in Naypyidaw. Dialogue, according to the United States, will supplement, rather than replace, decades of U.S. sanctions policy. These talks have already begun, and the United States has indicated that any improvement in relations between the two countries is possible only when Myanmar's military regime enacts meaningful and concrete reforms in the country, particularly in the areas of democracy and human rights.

On the other hand, in adjusting its policy towards Myanmar, the United States must face reality with a clear vision. Among other things, this vision must recognize that the United States' ability to help solve Myanmar's problems and to influence the course of the country's governance is extremely limited. American influence in Myanmar is unlikely to outweigh that of increasingly powerful Asian neighbours. Therefore, the United States' priority must be to clarify its fundamental objectives in Myanmar and follow them through consistently with some flexibility. Moreover, Myanmar is not likely to rank very high on the list of U.S. foreign policy priorities in the foreseeable future; so resources to address U.S. goals in Myanmar will be limited, compared with priority countries and regions.[1]

OBSERVATION OF THE MYANMAR IMPASSE: BREAKTHROUGH OR FALSE DAWN?

Recently, there have been signs of a thaw in U.S.-Myanmar relations in light of the Obama administration's policy review on Myanmar. In August 2009, Myanmar's State Peace and Development Council (SPDC) allowed Senator Jim Webb to visit and meet with the junta chair as well as with Daw Aung San Suu Kyi, leader of the National League for Democracy (NLD), and it subsequently released American John Yettaw who had been convicted of breaching security laws by sneaking into Suu Kyi's home. The release of more than 7,114 prisoners that included over a hundred political detainees and Prime Minister Thein Sein's attendance at the U.N. General Assembly (the first in fourteen years) are interpreted by many observers as conciliatory moves on the part of Myanmar in the face of demands to free all political prisoners and honour the (non-binding) U.N. resolutions on Myanmar. U.S. Secretary of State Hillary Clinton had expressed the view that both sanctions and engagement had failed to deliver what the West wanted and to choose one over the other was not helpful. And this was reiterated in her statement after the second "High-Level Meeting of the Group of Friends of Myanmar" convened by the United Nations Secretary-General (UNSG) on 23 September 2009, in which she mentioned, "Engagement versus sanctions is a false choice in our opinion. Going forward, we will be employing both of these tools."

This immediately caught the attention of the news media and hopes were raised, with Seth Mydans of the *New York Times* calling it the "most significant modification of administration policy towards Myanmar". In response, Suu Kyi's lawyer reported that she accepted direct engagement, but it must be on both sides, meaning engagement with both the government and the opposition. Kurt Campbell, Assistant Secretary of State for East Asian and Pacific Affairs, was later named as the point person for the U.S. initiative. In his press briefing, Campbell reiterated that the United States' core concerns regarding Myanmar remained unchanged, that the envisaged direct dialogue would include specific discussions of democracy and human rights inside Myanmar, and that cooperation on international security issues and areas of mutual benefit, such as counternarcotics, would remain. Whether this new engagement policy can herald the beginning of rapprochement between the United States and Myanmar, and whether the United States can successfully perform the difficult balancing act between carrot and stick in engaging Myanmar's military, depend on the military leaders' perception of the apparent U.S. policy change.

Despite the fact that the first real step to engage was initiated by Myanmar's interlocutors, which came with the impression that the regime was prepared to sit down with the United States, the big question was what was there for Myanmar's ruling generals to respond to positively. So long as sanctions continued unabated — with the United States reserving the option to apply additional targeted sanctions, if warranted — and the U.S. professed goal of implanting liberal democracy and assuring universal norms of human rights remained unchanged, what was portrayed as a significant concession from the American side could be seen as an empty gesture by Myanmar's leaders. The addition of proliferation issues and relations with the Democratic People's Republic of Korea (DPRK) in the dialogue would be viewed as uncomfortably close to the heart of the regime's security paradigm. To them, there are no real carrots and the stick is ineffective anyway. As for "high level" engagement between the two governments, the designated U.S. official may not be "high" enough to warrant a counterpart with substantive authority to negotiate on behalf of the powers that be in Myanmar.

Nevertheless, the dual-track policy is better for the long run than relying entirely on sanctions, smart or otherwise. But one should not conclude that the United States' move could lead to the immediate release of Suu Kyi and other political prisoners, or move the junta to negotiate for change towards acceptable modes of political and human rights practices (to the West). At best, one should regard this movement as a first small step towards a process of confidence building between the two governments. To this extent, Webb is not a lone wolf. Senior senators such as John Kerry and Richard Lugar, key figures in the Senate Committee on Foreign Relations, acknowledge the shortcomings of the current U.S. policy on Myanmar. Lugar previously broke ranks with his Republican Party on Cuba, calling for the normalization of diplomatic relations between the two countries.

As the moral dimensions of the Myanmar policy still looms large in Washington, advocates of new initiatives prefer behind-the-scenes approaches. Although the official position of the State Department is still intact, analysts within policy circles are busy calculating the positive and negative sides of the U.S. policy on Myanmar. The moral dimension of the current policy may become less significant, albeit not entirely dissipated. If U.S. national interest becomes the backbone of its new policy on Myanmar, Washington's policy shift concerning Naypyidaw would gain momentum.

A STRATEGIC PARADIGM SHIFT?

There are three major underlying reasons encompassing the United States' new policy towards Myanmar.

Under President Obama, the most fundamental deviation from the Bush administration's foreign policy is the recognition of the limit of U.S. power in the world. The Bush administration's neo-conservative world view called for the use of U.S. power to bring about freedom and democracy. In contrast, Obama and his strategic advisors acknowledge that the extension of U.S. power has reached a critical threshold. Indeed, the United States has become a relatively declining power in the face of a rising China, Russia, and India. Although the United States is still the most powerful nation militarily, the American economy is largely interdependent with the Asian economy. China holds the largest percentage of U.S. debt. The combination of Japanese and Chinese ownership of U.S. debt has reached 45 per cent of U.S. Treasury securities. With its seemingly declining power, the United States realizes that the most effective approach in the handling of foreign relations will be the utilization of soft power, which calls for friendliness rather than coercion. Under a new strategic paradigm, Obama has seemed to refrain from highlighting democracy promotion from his country's major foreign policy agenda. He carefully avoided the word "democracy" in his inaugural speech. In contrast, he explicitly proclaimed that the United States would reach out to non-democracies rather than preaching to them the merits of political transformation in the interests of the United States. This new strategic perspective also shapes the U.S. policy shift towards Myanmar.

THE ROLE OF ASEAN

Another strategy shift has been the United States' new perspective on ASEAN. The Bush administration considered ASEAN as a less strategic region compared with the Middle East, except in the case of the war on terror. The Bush administration refused to sign the Treaty of Amity and Cooperation (TAC), which requires all signatories to refrain from using military force against other signatory states. Additionally, Myanmar has long been a thorn in

U.S.-ASEAN relations. The Bush administration promoted more bilateral relations with major non-NATO allies such as Thailand and the Philippines, rather than multilateral cooperation with the region as a whole. While the United States kept its distance from ASEAN, China launched an efficacious charm offensive in the region. In the aftermath of the Asian financial crisis in 1997, China came to the rescue of some ASEAN members, thus winning their hearts and minds. Moreover, China's ratification of the TAC pacified the fear of some ASEAN countries concerning the rise of the dragon. ASEAN, as a consequence, has grown increasingly comfortable with China. China's total trade with ASEAN has also grown by 1,034 per cent since 1995. Meanwhile, the growth of ASEAN's trade with the United States stood at a mere 75 per cent.

The new administration in Washington has apparently felt China's strong inroads into the region. Bilateral relations simply cannot preserve waning U.S. influence in Southeast Asia; hence, it has to embrace ASEAN as a whole. As a result, Washington acceded to the TAC on 22 July 2009. If the United States aims at moving closer to ASEAN, the Myanmar issue cannot be allowed to serve as a stumbling block.

THE CHINA FACTOR

The Sino-Myanmar relationship will enter a new chapter after China completes an oil pipeline connecting the Andaman Sea with its Yunnan province, a truly strategic move in the eyes of leaders in Beijing. The projected oil pipeline through Myanmar will reinforce China's long-term strategic energy security. The pipeline in Myanmar will be a plausible reason for China to send its advanced submarines to the Andaman Sea to protect its strategic interest, simultaneously restricting the regional power projection of the U.S. Navy's 7th fleet.

Although the United States is militarily capable of neutralizing China's land-based pipeline and pumping stations in Myanmar, any military action involving a third country in an event of direct confrontation between the United States and China will be politically complicated — especially since the United States' recent accession to the TAC effectively limits Washington's potential countermeasures. Once a moral issue, Myanmar is now being perceived by the United States as part of its security and national interests.

FUTURE DIRECTION AND CONTENTIOUS ISSUES

When Senator Webb visited Myanmar in August 2009, the reception given to him at Naypyidaw was very enthusiastic, as reported in this excerpt:[2]

> There is no doubt that in recent months, the junta began to court the West, especially the United States. The recent high-profile visit of the American Senator Jim Webb clearly showed the junta's interest in engaging Washington. His reception in the capital, Naypyidaw, was on par with that which is strictly reserved for visiting heads of state, according to diplomats based in Yangon. And his welcome was even more enthusiastic than that given to the U.N. Secretary General, Ban Ki-moon, when he visited Myanmar in July. Myanmar's neighbours and fellow members of the regional grouping ASEAN have also been encouraging the junta to seize the opportunity to reach out to Washington as it reviewed its overall policy and strategy towards the military regime. Singapore, in particular, has been at the forefront of this move. But while the generals may be keen to improve relations with the United States, they are also keen to have sanctions lifted. As the international economic crisis and credit crunch begins to bite, they are anxious to reduce the impact sanctions have had on the country. What Washington offers for talks with the regime may yet determine how successful this shift in U.S. policy will be. "Words are not enough," said [Derek] Tonkin [former British ambassador to Thailand and Vietnam]. "The United States needs to make some concrete gesture, like removing sanctions which seriously affect people, like the embargo on garment exports."

On 8 June 2010, Webb sent a letter to Secretary of State Clinton regarding his recent trip to Asia and his recommendations for strengthening U.S. policy in the region. Among other issues, Myanmar was one of his concerns. He said:

> In May 2010, Assistant Secretary of State Kurt Campbell raised allegations that Myanmar has violated its commitment to the UN Resolution 1874 regarding acceptance of shipments of military items from North Korea. Although not explained in his statement, and not validated by subsequent information, news reports alleged that Myanmar received a shipment of arms from North Korea. This allegation which, from my understanding, has yet to be publicly clarified and substantiated by the State Department, has frozen any prospect of further engagement with the Myanmar government. Prior to my recent Asia trip, I and my staff worked for weeks to seek public clarification of this allegation, but the State Department provided none. At the time I left for my trip to Asia, no other countries had joined the United States in this allegation, although it had been discussed with several countries. The State Department still has not publicly clarified this matter. My staff was told by Deputy Assistant Secretary of State Scot Marciel that no other nation has joined the United States in publicly denouncing Myanmar on this matter. As you know, only hours before I was scheduled to enter Burma/Myanmar, reports surfaced in the international media regarding new allegations that the military regime was cooperating with North Korea to develop a nuclear program. These allegations were raised by the Democratic Voice of Burma, a U.S.-funded media organization. As a consequence, I postponed my visit to Myanmar until such time as both of them can be examined objectively and factually. I am now calling on you to do so, in a timely manner, so that our future relations with this country can proceed forward in a responsible way."[3]

On 11 June 2010, as international media were reporting allegations that Myanmar had been attempting to develop a nuclear programme in collaboration with North Korea with an aim to acquire nuclear weapons, Myanmar's Foreign Ministry, while rebutting the groundless allegations, clarified this point:

> Following the adoption of the U.S. government's engagement policy towards Myanmar, Senator Jim Webb and Assistant Secretary of State Kurt Campbell visited Myanmar and started the engagement process between the two countries. At a time of resumption of engagement between Myanmar and the United States, those unfounded allegations were made up by the anti-government elements in collaboration with news media with political purpose in a timely manner. Besides, it was also an attempt to tarnish the image of the Myanmar government and to disrupt its on-going political process at a time when the government is exerting all out efforts to holding general elections for democratic transformation. As a result of surfacing of those allegations, Senator Jim Webb who was scheduled to visit Myanmar in early June has postponed his planned visit.[4]

Engagement: Real or Lip-Service?

Regardless of policy perspectives, the U.S. engagement with Myanmar's military government will be quite different from the way in which ASEAN does business. Democratization and human rights will still be a part of U.S. policy goals in Myanmar. But the United States has dropped some major preconditions for initial engagement, such as the release of Suu Kyi and all political prisoners. In the near future, the two countries will likely experience a quid pro quo engagement, ranging from counternarcotics to political prisoners (Suu Kyi was finally released on 13 November 2010). Among all initiatives in the past year, the focus of U.S. policy was on the 2010 elections.

This was a major shift from the Bush administration, which adamantly demanded that transition in Myanmar must come through a negotiated settlement between the government, the NLD, and the ethnic nationalities. While America's new policy will hail any conciliatory settlement between the opposition and the government, Washington will no longer hold its breath on a dialogue-driven transition in Myanmar. The United States, in the post-election period, has not yet acknowledged a military-led transition in the country, even after the new government released Suu Kyi a week after the election.

The most crucial issue of U.S. policy on Myanmar pertained to the legitimacy of the 2010 election. Washington did not want to abandon its moral code altogether, and thus would need a plausible reason to facilitate its policy shift on Myanmar. A legitimate election would allow the United States to move closer to Myanmar in the near future. But unfortunately this was not the case. Some observers believed that the election may alter Myanmar's political landscape for decades to come. Concurrently, Myanmar's relationship with the United States will depend on the political development in the post-election period. If the new government is capable of addressing international concerns on human rights issues, Myanmar's relationship with the United States could gradually improve.[5]

ASEAN'S VIEW ON THE SHIFT OF U.S. POLICY

The change in the U.S. position has been unanimously welcomed in the region. At the first ASEAN-U.S. Leaders' Meeting held in Singapore on 15 November 2009, a joint statement was issued, including this passage:

> The Leaders of ASEAN welcomed the high level dialogue and the policy of the United States to engage with the Government of Myanmar, as indicated by the recent visit of U.S. officials to Myanmar. We expressed our hope that this effort, as well as ASEAN's, would contribute to broad political and economic reforms and the process will be further enhanced in the future. We also underscored the importance of achieving national reconciliation and that the general elections to be held in Myanmar in 2010 must be conducted in a free, fair, inclusive and transparent

manner in order to be credible to the international community. We called on the Government of Myanmar to help create the conditions for credible elections including by initiating a dialogue with all stakeholders to ensure that the process is fully inclusive. We also reiterated our continued support to the good offices of the United Nations Secretary-General in the democratization process in Myanmar. We also noted the Joint Communiqué of the 42nd ASEAN Foreign Ministers Meeting in Phuket, 20 July 2009.[6]

Previously, at the 42nd ASEAN Foreign Ministers Meeting held at Phuket, Thailand, on 20 July 2009, the joint communiqué stated:

We took note of the briefing by Myanmar on the recent visit of the United Nations Secretary-General Ban Ki-moon to Myanmar. We encouraged the Myanmar Government to hold free, fair and inclusive elections in 2010, thereby laying down a good foundation for future social and economic development. In this regard, recalling the ASEAN Leaders' Statement on 19 November 2007, we reiterated our calls on the Government of Myanmar to immediately release all those under detention, including Daw Aung San Suu Kyi, thereby paving [the] way for genuine reconciliation and meaningful dialogue involving all parties concerned and with a view to enabling them to participate in the 2010 General Elections.[7]

Myanmar expressed its view that pressure from the outside and economic sanctions were hampering Myanmar's democratization and development efforts. Recognizing the fact that the Myanmar Government has been trying to address many complex challenges, we remained constructively engaged with Myanmar as part of the ASEAN Community building process. We continued to support the ongoing good offices of the United Nations Secretary-General and welcomed Myanmar's assurances to cooperate fully with the United Nations.[8]

Prior to the political transition, many ASEAN members refrained from commenting on the new election laws in Myanmar. Only two have openly rebuked this law and its implications. "Unless they release Aung San Suu Kyi and allow her and her party to participate in the elections, it's a complete farce and therefore contrary to their road map to democracy", said Foreign Secretary Alberto Romulo of the Philippines.[9] Likewise, Teuku Faizasyah, a spokesman of Indonesia's Foreign Ministry, said that the law may undermine the election because it will result in an election that is not inclusive.[10]

Early in February 2010, ASEAN's Secretary-General Surin Pitsuwan told the BBC's *Hardtalk* that ASEAN expected a credible and transparent election in Myanmar in 2010, but it cannot interfere in the details of the election. Surin emphasized, "No election is perfect. It has to begin. That's why they [the Myanmar regime] are beginning. They promise [to hold an election] at the end of this year." He also added that the Myanmar generals' commitment to the election should be seen as a positive factor.[11]

Notes

1. Asia Society Task Force, *Current Realities and Future Possibilities in Burma/Myanmar: Options for U.S. Policy*, March 2010, p. 8 <http://asiasociety.org/files/pdf/ASBurma/MyanmarMyanmar_TaskForceReport.pdf> (accessed 12 July 2010).

2. Larry Jagan, "U.S. Policy Shift on Burma/Myanmar Gets Mixed Reactions", Inter Press Service, 25 September 2009 <http://ipsnews.net/news.asp?idnews=48589> (accessed 12 July 2010).

3. "Webb Recommends State Department Strengthen Engagement in Asia", 8 June 2010 <http://webb.senate.gov/newsroom/pressreleases/2010-06-08-01.cfm> (accessed 12 July 2010).

4. "Press Statement of Ministry of Foreign Affairs on Unfounded Allegations against Myanmar regarding Nuclear Program", The Ministry of Foreign Affairs, Nay Pyi Taw, Union of Myanmar, 11 June 2010 <http://www.mofa.gov.mm/pressrelease/Press%20Statement%20of%20Ministry%20of%20Foreign%20Affairs%20on%20unfounded.htm> (accessed 12 July 2010).

5. Min Zaw Oo, "Inevitable U.S. Policy Shift on Burma/Myanmar: Why and How", Mizzima News, 7 September 2009 <http://www.mizzima.com/edop/commentary/2729-inevitable-us-policy-shift-on-Burma/Myanmar-why-and-how-.html> (accessed 12 July 2010).

6. "Joint Statement — 1st ASEAN-U.S. Leaders' Meeting", ASEAN Secretariat, Paragraph 10, 15 November 2009 <http://www.aseansec.org/24020.htm> (accessed 12 July 2010).

7. "Joint Communiqué of the 42nd ASEAN Foreign Ministers Meeting", *ASEAN Secretariat*,

Paragraph 68, 20 July 2009 <http://www.irrawaddy.org/article.php?art_id=18044> (accessed 12 July 2010).

8. Ibid., Paragraph 69.

9. "Burma's Leaders Annul Suu Kyi's 1990 Poll Win", BBC News, 11 March 2010 <http://news.bbc.co.uk/2/hi/asia-pacific/8561354.stm> (accessed 12 July 2010).

10. Wai Moe, "ASEAN's Silence on Burmese Election Law", *The Irrawaddy*, 15 March 2010 <http://www.irrawaddy.org/article.php?art_id=18044> (accessed 12 July 2010).

11. Ibid.

11

UNITED STATES ASSISTANCE TO ASEAN THROUGH THE ADVANCE PROGRAMME

Jennifer Collier Wilson

The United States is deeply committed to supporting ASEAN and its goal of creating the ASEAN Community by 2015. For over thirty years, the United States has been a faithful dialogue partner, working closely with ASEAN to implement a wide range of projects and programmes that have supported growth, security, democracy, and prosperity in the region.

The basis for ASEAN-U.S cooperation is the Joint Vision Statement on the ASEAN-U.S. Enhanced Partnership (AEP) that was simultaneously issued in all ASEAN capitals and in Washington D.C. in 2005. This document sets out the broad goals for the ASEAN-U.S. relationship. It provides for cooperation across all three of ASEAN's pillars to promote an "open and outward looking, dynamic and resilient ASEAN Community".

To implement the AEP, ASEAN and the United States developed the ASEAN-U.S. Enhanced Partnership Plan of Action in 2006. This document identified specific, actionable programmes that could be implemented to promote the broad goals of the AEP. The first plan of action operates for five years, expiring in 2011. ASEAN and the United States are currently in the process of developing a new plan of action to cover the period from 2011 to 2016, to be finalized in mid-2011. As called for in the AEP, the United States and ASEAN negotiated and signed the United States–ASEAN Trade and Investment Framework Arrangement in 2006 that provides further structure for cooperation on economic matters.

Over the past two and a half years, the Obama administration has sought to further expand and enhance the U.S. relationship with ASEAN. Secretary of State Hillary Rodham Clinton, on her first trip outside the United States as Secretary of State, visited the ASEAN Secretariat in February 2009 and said, "This region is vital to the future of not only the United States and each of the countries, but to the world's common interests." She noted that ASEAN embodies "a set of countries that will be key to any solutions we pursue on climate change, counter-terrorism, global health, and so much else".

Since then, the United States has acceded to the Treaty of Amity and Cooperation in Southeast Asia, announced the opening of a new U.S. Mission to ASEAN based in Jakarta, with a resident ambassador to ASEAN, and President Obama participated in the first-ever ASEAN-U.S. leaders meeting with all ten ASEAN heads of government in November 2009. At that meeting, the leaders of the ASEAN member states and the United States agreed to a joint declaration that sets out priority areas of cooperation for 2010 in millions.

U.S. ASSISTANCE TO ASEAN

The ASEAN-U.S. Enhanced Partnership laid the foundation for a comprehensive programme of assistance to ASEAN, and increased focus on the region under the Obama administration forms the backdrop for the current activities. American support for the region comes in a number of forms. Figure 11.1 below sets out the amounts

FIGURE 11.1

U.S Direct Development Assistance in Southeast Asia in 2008 (millions)

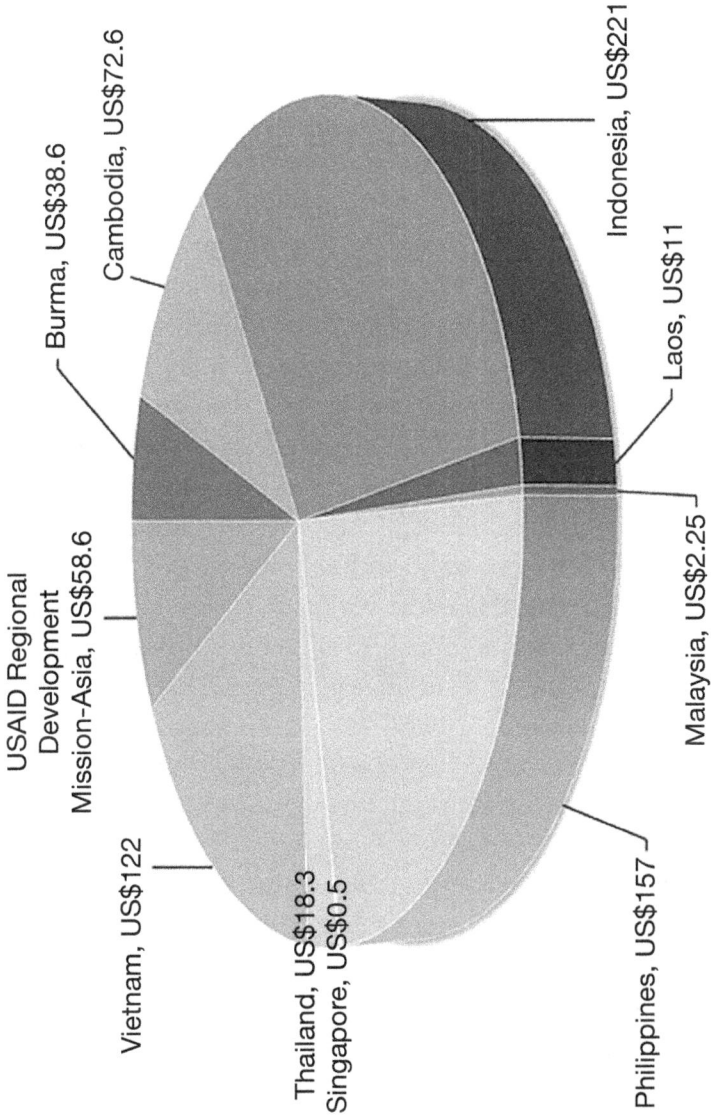

Cambodia, US$72.6

Burma, US$38.6

Indonesia, US$221

Laos, US$11

USAID Regional Development Mission-Asia, US$58.6

Malaysia, US$2.25

Vietnam, US$122

Thailand, US$18.3
Singapore, US$0.5

Philippines, US$157

of direct development assistance that the United States provided in the region in 2008.

ADVANCE

A cornerstone for support to ASEAN is the ASEAN Development Vision to Advance National Cooperation Program, known as ADVANCE.[1] Launched by the U.S. Agency for International Development (USAID) and the U.S. State Department in October 2007, ADVANCE is an umbrella programme that provides core support to ASEAN. ADVANCE was established to deliver targeted, quick-response technical assistance at regional, subregional, and bilateral levels, in collaboration with the ASEAN Secretariat and member states, and to support public and private sector integration in the ASEAN region. ADVANCE is designed to strengthen the ASEAN Secretariat as an institution and provide assistance in integration across all three pillars of ASEAN — political-security community, economic community, and socio-cultural community.

The long-term impact of this assistance will be increased responsiveness of ASEAN to its member states through a strengthened secretariat and consultative processes. This in turn will help ASEAN to fulfil its regional mandate better through strengthened institutional capacity to manage daily affairs and address development needs of member states. Working together on shared development priorities is a key priority of U.S. engagement with ASEAN. Continued integration among ASEAN member states will improve the region's ability to be competitive in the global marketplace and will help address trans-boundary and global challenges.

In addition, regional integration will help to narrow the development gap between member states. ASEAN plays a crucial role in advocating national level efforts to improve the lives of citizens in its member states through improved governance, investments in education and health, and sustainable and balanced economic growth. The ASEAN platform offers an opportunity to share knowledge and best practices among member states and build consensus on the best approaches for positive development outcomes.

Core funding for ADVANCE comes from USAID and the U.S. State Department. Other U.S. government agencies can and do fund activities that are implemented through ADVANCE. Current planned funding is about US$38 million over five years.

Four projects are currently operating under the ADVANCE umbrella:

1) ASEAN-U.S. Technical Assistance and Training Facility
2) ASEAN Single Window Project
3) ASEAN Value Chain Project
4) Lao Bilateral Trade Agreement (BTA) Implementation/World Trade Organization (WTO) Accession Project

ASEAN-U.S. Technical Assistance and Training Facility

The ASEAN-U.S. Technical Assistance and Training Facility promotes the goals of the ASEAN-U.S. Enhanced Partnership Plan of Action and the Trade and Investment Framework Arrangement (TIFA), while supporting ASEAN's own vision, encapsulated in the road map for an ASEAN Community, to create an outward-looking, stable, peaceful, and prosperous ASEAN Community.

The facility provides support to:

- Improve regional responses to transnational issues, including counterterrorism, money laundering, trafficking in persons, and trafficking in illicit drugs;
- Enhance ASEAN economic and financial integration and cooperation;
- Expand regional cooperation in disaster management, public health, and other human development issues; and
- Strengthen the ASEAN Secretariat's ability to provide support for the establishment of the ASEAN Community.

The facility began operations under ADVANCE in October 2007 and will continue until September 2012. It is based in the ASEAN Secretariat in Jakarta and conducts activities across all three ASEAN pillars, as well as provides support for the development of the ASEAN Secretariat.

Current and planned major areas of collaboration between the facility and ASEAN include transnational crime (including trafficking in persons and financial crimes); human rights; ASEAN Regional Forum; trade facilitation (including customs and standards); food security; environment and climate change; disaster management (including pandemic preparedness and response); labour/migration; and education.

Current highlights of facility activities include:

- Working with regional experts to establish the Human Rights Resource Centre; supporting training for the ASEAN Intergovernmental Commission on Human Rights;
- Training for customs officials in Cambodia, Laos, and Vietnam on how to identify and curb bulk cash smuggling;
- Publishing with ISEAS: *Realizing the ASEAN Economic Community: A Comprehensive Assessment;*
- Sponsoring the ASEAN Food Security Conference to engage the private sector in the ASEAN Integrated Food Security Framework;
- Developing a repository of migrant labour laws and regulations to promote and protect migrant labour rights in the region;
- Advising the secretariat on options to develop an ASEAN Volunteers Programme;
- Conducting regional workshops for ASEAN member state officials on climate change related to floods and droughts; and
- Promoting ASEAN awareness curriculum development and ASEAN studies programme development in cooperation with the ASEAN University Network

ASEAN Single Window Project

The ASEAN Single Window (ASW) Project began in 2008 and will continue till 2013. Its objective is to support ASEAN's effort to implement the ASW, an integrated system of National Single Windows in ASEAN member states that provides a single point of data entry and electronic clearance for importers and exporters to fulfil border procedures. An integrated system will allow faster clearance of shipments and improved enforcement by government agencies.

The project focuses on the following activities:

*   Technical Support: providing technical assistance to support a regional ASW architecture linking ASEAN National Single Windows (NSWs).
*   Legal Support: developing legal foundations for operation of the ASW. The project helped draft an ASW Legal Framework Agreement and related documentation and is conducting single window legal gap analyses and capacity building activities to improve understanding of the legal issues involved.
*   NSW Support: supporting the establishment of National Single Windows of newer ASEAN member states, focusing currently on Vietnam and Laos.
*   Private Sector Outreach: supporting private sector outreach and public awareness related to the ASW.

Current highlights of the ASW project include:

*   The ASW Pilot Project to test the technical environment for the electronic exchange of information between the National Single Windows of ASEAN member states.
*   Data Harmonization through the development of the ASEAN Data Model (ADM), which harmonizes data requirements for regulatory and commercial documents (e.g., bill of lading,

manifest, e-certificate, phytosanitary certificate, etc.), using international standards.

- Certificate of Origin and Customs Declaration Document Applications. Indonesia, Malaysia, and the Philippines (and soon, Brunei) are already electronically exchanging the origin certificate required to benefit from reduced duties in the context of the ASEAN Free Trade Area agreement (CEPT Form D), which they believe has cut down origin fraud significantly. The project also assisted in the development of a software application for the ASEAN Customs Declaration Document, which is used for both export and import declarations, and will help expedite goods clearance at borders, thus facilitating trade for compliant traders.

- Legal gap analyses to review a country's laws, regulations, decrees, etc., to identify legal issues in e-commerce and the electronic exchange of cross-border transaction data, such as data confidentiality, information security, electronic signatures, authentication, liability, data retention and archiving, dispute resolution, and intellectual property rights. The first legal gap analysis was undertaken in Vietnam, with further plans in Laos and the Philippines.

ASEAN Value Chain Project

USAID is also supporting enhanced regional integration of selected ASEAN priority integration sectors. In the Economic Community Blueprint, ASEAN identified twelve priority sectors for accelerated integration. In a programme begun in 2008 and running until 2013, ADVANCE is providing assistance to priority industry sectors, in conjunction with regional business associations, to improve integration of cross-border supply chains. The overall objective is increased intraregional trade through identifying and removing constraints in the business environment that affect ASEAN's competitiveness and integration in these sectors.

For example, USAID has worked with the ASEAN Federation of Textile Industries (AFTEX) to connect manufacturers throughout the region through leading-edge initiatives in supply chain integration, quality standards, and human resource development. The Source ASEAN Full Service Alliance (SAFSA) programme unites textile mills and garment factories to form virtual vertical factories that provide the full service required by global apparel buyers. To ensure that these customers receive the quality services and products they expect, the project has worked with AFTEX to develop SAFSA quality service standards that will be professionally certified. ASEAN's garment workforce will also benefit from the ASEAN Common Competency Programme under which AFTEX will certify garment worker qualifications that will be mutually recognized throughout ASEAN.

Lao BTA Implementation/WTO Accession Project

USAID provides technical assistance and training to help the Government of Laos and local stakeholders to advance efforts to modernize and deepen Laos' legal system and to liberalize its trade and investment regime, consistent with commitments under the U.S.-Lao BTA, WTO accession, and the ASEAN Economic Community Blueprint. The project began in 2007 and has been extended until September 2011 and significantly expanded. A key element of the expansion was the posting of a full-time resident project director and trade advisor in Vientiane.

The project focuses on the following:

- Transparency: informing and involving key stakeholders in the domestic reform and liberalization process; ensuring accessibility to trade related materials, laws, regulations, and agreements.
- Legal and Economic Analysis: promoting understanding within the government and among other key stakeholders of

the economic benefits of international agreements, as well as their obligations; building capacity to formulate trade policy and regulations.

- Raising Awareness: fostering exchanges to highlight the adjustments necessary for, and the benefits of, increased competition in the Lao market and increased access to export markets.

Current highlights of the project include:

- A seminar held on advancing public-private policy dialogue on trade negotiations
- A study mission to Vietnam organized for a cross-agency team led by the Ministry of Industry and Commerce to learn how Vietnam managed its BTA implementation and WTO accession.
- Submission of a comprehensive Intellectual Property Rights (IPR) Assessment to the relevant government officials for comment and definition of further support areas, including the development of the implementing decree for a new IPR Law, developing action plans for acceding to the Berne Convention on Copyrights and the International Union for the Protection of New Varieties of Plants (UPOV) convention on protecting plant varieties, and supporting the completion of the first patent approvals in Laos.
- Updating of the legislative agenda for implementing the U.S.-Lao Bilateral Trade Agreement, comments on customs valuation regulations, and support for developing the first draft of the implementing decree for a new standards law.

Note

1. ADVANCE is implemented by a consortium of twenty-six U.S. and ASEAN regional companies and organizations, led by Nathan Associates of Arlington, Virginia.

12

CONCLUSION

Pavin Chachavalpongpun

In July 2010, the ASEAN Studies Centre of the Institute of Southeast Asian Studies organized a workshop on ASEAN-United States relations. The workshop entertained lively discussions on topics related to the overall theme — what are the talking points?

In the first session, on political cooperation, the issue of the South China Sea dominated the discussion. Here are some of the comments and questions:

- The United States has a major stake in the region's peace and stability. But it has no clear policy on the South China Sea. So far, Washington has seemed to adopt a non-interference policy with regard to the territorial dispute in the South China Sea. Can the United States really stay out of the current conflict when, in fact, the conflict may pose a threat to its interest in the region? The United States has over the years forged a close military alliance with certain members of ASEAN through a series of military exercises. Will such exercises permit the United States to play a role in the South China Sea? U.S. Defence Minister Robert Gates once said that the United States was willing to help countries in the region to step up their naval capacity and to support them in preventing the tension in the South China Sea from developing into a real threat.

- China has never had a well-defined policy with regard to the South China Sea. But this ambiguity is beneficial for China as it negotiates with other claimants.

- The strength of the U.S. Navy peaked during the Cold War, but has gradually declined since. This coincided with the modernization of the People's Liberation Army (PLA) of China. In the meantime, Southeast Asia has increasingly become a "vulnerable flashpoint" as maritime terrorism continues to challenge regional peace and security. How will the United States and rising China use their available resources to cope with that threat?

- Has the U.S. presence in Southeast Asia been used to counter China's military modernization? A Chinese scholar raised this question: What would be the United States' option in view of China's increasingly modernized army/navy? He also commented that China's military rise was a natural phenomenon, after long years of economic growth. Moreover, the shift in the balance of power in the region seems to be in China's favour. China has come to fill the leadership vacuum.

- A Singaporean commentator agreed with the above assertion, emphasizing that it would not be in Southeast Asia's interest to adopt an antagonistic policy towards China. In return, China's military modernization would at a certain level encourage leaders in Beijing to open up their policy, making it more transparent, in order to weaken the image of China's threat.

- ASEAN's Defence Ministers Meeting (ADMM), a platform that will also include the involvement of the United States, represents another alternative for ASEAN to engage with outside powers. But participants in the workshop mostly agreed that while ADMM may not have a fixed agenda and will only discuss issues deemed "necessary for the day", it provides a venue for country participants to meet on a regular basis.

• Participants engaged in a debate on what constituted China's core interests. They asked, "Has China really made the territorial claim over the South China Sea part of protecting its core interests?" While other core interests are obvious, including Taiwan, Tibet, and Xinjiang, claiming sovereignty over the South China Sea has remained largely obscure. If China is willing to use force in the case of the South China Sea in order to protect its so-called core interest, then China will be breaching the Declaration on the Conduct of Parties in the South China Sea which it signed with ASEAN in 2002.

• One participant from China clarified that China has never made the South China Sea a part of its core interests. Whatever the Chinese media (Xinhua) reported has never been confirmed by the state authority. In reality, China is keen to cooperate with the United States, especially on the South China Sea issue.

• Bo Zhiyue of the East Asia Institute asserted that Deng Xiaoping always believed that sovereignty was non-negotiable. But Bo asked, "What was the border of Chinese sovereignty?" Therefore, while China may appear to seek cooperation with other claimants on joint development of the territory in dispute in the South China Sea, it has never really changed its view of sovereignty as defined by Deng.

In the session on strategic issues, "Myanmar" dominated the discussion. Tin Maung Maung Than of ISEAS said that the elections in Myanmar would bring a new set of power players, especially if Senior General Than Shwe, chairman of the State Peace and Development Council (SPDC), would not contest the elections. Other participants agreed that it was likely that ASEAN would endorse the elections, which may be free, but not fair. As for Sino-Myanmar relations, while they may not change much after the elections, a question will emerge: How will Myanmar's new government deal with the ethnic problem and make sure it will not have an undesirable impact on China? In the view of Myint Soe, visiting senior research fellow at ISEAS, economic reform would be more easily attainable compared with political reform. The question of whether Myanmar has been developing its nuclear programme gained much attention from the audience. Tin concluded that the answer lay in the scientific capacity of Myanmar, rather than in the real capacity of the Tatmadaw, or Myanmar's army.

In the final session on human resource development, Jennifer Wilson of USAID asserted that U.S. technical assistance to ASEAN was apolitical. In countries such as Myanmar, the U.S. agency made sure that assistance would not be politicized. In the aftermath of Cyclone Nargis, the United States' humanitarian assistance had been given to Myanmar's Government and its rehabilitation programme was still ongoing.

In sum, one of the main findings of this workshop is that ASEAN has remained very important for the United States and vice versa, albeit in different ways. The discussion covered a wide range of topics. Participants were interested in issues such as maritime security and free navigation; and it was not just physical freedom, but included the freedom to exchange goods without a multitude of obstacles. The ASEAN market is significant to the United States, but this significance is diminishing simply because ASEAN has not been as integrated as government officials described it.

Some difficult issues, for example, democratization in Myanmar, have, to a certain extent, obstructed development of ties between ASEAN and the United States. However, one should understand that the U.S. policy towards Myanmar has been primarily shaped by domestic factors. Ultimately, leaders of ASEAN and in Washington recognize the need to strengthen their relations further, despite the existing problem of Myanmar and the rising influence of China, as reflected in the U.S. nomination of a resident ambassador to ASEAN and its commitment to attend future summits with ASEAN leaders.

INDEX

127